South Africa
in World History

The
New
Oxford
World
History

South Africa
in World History

Iris Berger

OXFORD
UNIVERSITY PRESS

2009

OXFORD
UNIVERSITY PRESS

Oxford University Press, Inc., publishes works that further
Oxford University's objective of excellence
in research, scholarship, and education.

Oxford   New York
Auckland   Cape Town   Dar es Salaam   Hong Kong   Karachi
Kuala Lumpur   Madrid   Melbourne   Mexico City   Nairobi
New Delhi   Shanghai   Taipei   Toronto

With offices in
Argentina   Austria   Brazil   Chile   Czech Republic   France   Greece
Guatemala   Hungary   Italy   Japan   Poland   Portugal   Singapore
South Korea   Switzerland   Thailand   Turkey   Ukraine   Vietnam

Copyright © 2009 by Oxford University Press, Inc.

Published by Oxford University Press, Inc.
198 Madison Avenue, New York, NY 10016

www.oup.com

Oxford is a registered trademark of Oxford University Press

Library of Congress Cataloging-in-Publication Data
Berger, Iris.
South Africa in world history / Iris Berger.
p. cm. — (The new Oxford world history)
Includes bibliographical references and index.
Summary: "Discusses the history of South Africa from the early centuries
of the Common Era to the present day and addresses broad themes of world history
such as colonialism, white settlement, nationalism and reconciliation"
—Provided by publisher.
ISBN 978-0-19-515754-3 (hardcover)—ISBN 978-0-19-533793-8 (pbk.)
1. South Africa—History.   I. Title.
DT1787.B47   2009
968—dc22   2008036666

Printed in the United States of America
on acid-free paper

*Frontispiece: Archbishop Desmond Tutu, head of the Truth and Reconciliation Commission,
and Alex Boraine, commissioner, greeting witnesses at the first hearing of the
commission on April 15, 1996, in East London. AP Photo / Mike Hutchings.*

For Leo

Contents

Editors' Preface

This book is part of the New Oxford World History, an innovative series that offers readers an informed, lively, and up-to-date history of the world and its people that represents a significant change from the "old" world history. Only a few years ago, world history generally amounted to a history of the West—Europe and the United States—with small amounts of information about the rest of the world. Some versions of the old world history drew attention to every part of the world *except* Europe and the United States. Readers of that kind of world history might get the impression that somehow the rest of the world was made up of exotic people who had strange customs and spoke difficult languages. Still another kind of "old" world history presented the story of areas or peoples of the world by focusing primarily on the achievements of great civilizations. Readers learned of great buildings, influential world religions, and mighty rulers but little of ordinary people or more general economic and social patterns. Interactions among the world's peoples were often told from only one perspective.

This series has a different perspective on world history. First, it is comprehensive, covering all countries and regions of the world and investigating the total human experience—even those of so-called "peoples without histories" living far from the great civilizations. "New" world historians thus share an interest in all of human history, even going back millions of years before there were written human records. A few "new" world histories even extend their focus to the entire universe, a "big history" perspective that dramatically shifts the beginning of the story back to the Big Bang. Some see the "new" global framework of world history today in terms of viewing the world from the vantage point of the moon, as one scholar put it. We agree. But we also want to take a close-up view, analyzing and reconstructing the significant experiences of all of humanity.

This is not to say that everything that has happened everywhere and in all time periods can be recovered or is worth knowing, but that there is much to be gained by considering both the separate and interrelated stories of different societies and cultures. Making these connections is still another crucial ingredient of the "new" world history. It emphasizes connectedness and interactions of all kinds—cultural, economic, political, religious, and social—involving peoples, places, and processes. It makes comparisons and finds similarities. Emphasizing both the comparisons and interactions is critical to developing a global framework that can deepen and broaden historical understanding, whether the focus is on a specific country or region or on the whole world.

The rise of the new world history as a discipline comes at an opportune time. The interest in world history in schools and among the general public is vast. We travel to one another's nations, converse and work with people around the world, and are changed by global events. War and peace affect populations worldwide as do economic conditions and the state of our environment, communications, and health and medicine. The New Oxford World History presents local histories in a global context and provides an overview of world events seen through the eyes of ordinary people. This combination of the local and the global further defines the new world history. Understanding the workings of global and local conditions in the past enables us to examine our own world and to envision the interconnected future that is in the making.

Bonnie G. Smith
Anand Yang

Preface

On June 6, 1966, Senator Robert F. Kennedy, brother of the late President John F. Kennedy, delivered a speech at the University of Cape Town. Kennedy spoke at the invitation of the National Union of South African Students. He began his remarks with an apparently straightforward summary of South African history. "I came here because of my deep interest and affection for a land settled by the Dutch in the mid-seventeenth century, then taken over by the British, and at last independent; a land in which the native inhabitants were at first subdued, but relations with whom remain a problem to this day; a land which defined itself on a hostile frontier; a land which has tamed rich natural resources through the energetic application of modern technology; a land which once imported slaves, and now must struggle to wipe out the last traces of that former bondage." His conclusion was unexpected, however. "I refer, of course, to the United States of America."

In establishing these common ties between the two countries, Kennedy was calling on young people to stand up against injustice and inhumanity across the globe. But his remarks also help to situate South Africa in the broader context of world history by placing it among the numerous countries colonized by Europeans as they swept across the globe from the late fifteenth century onward seeking new sources of wealth and power. As Kennedy observed, these conquests left a legacy of oppression, enslavement, and racial inequality combined with intense exploitation of natural resources and highly developed modern technology. As in Canada, Australia, New Zealand, and many countries in Latin America, South Africa attracted substantial numbers of European settlers who seized vast areas of land and appropriated valuable resources. In Africa, this South African narrative of dispossession paralleled the history of Southern Rhodesia (now Zimbabwe), Kenya, and Algeria. Kennedy also referred to the struggle to eradicate the final vestiges of bondage. Although the fight against apartheid was still ongoing in 1966, South Africa, unlike the United States, achieved its freedom through a combination of political, diplomatic, and military pressure rather than through a full-scale anticolonial war.

Despite its title, this book is too brief to explore in depth the connections and comparisons between South Africa and the rest of the world.

I have tried, however, to highlight some of these parallels as well as the close connections between black South Africans and African Americans. Drawing on a generation of pioneering research in social history, I have also sought to explore how South Africans of different racial, ethnic, and class backgrounds have both clashed and cooperated throughout the country's past and, unlike many historical syntheses, to integrate the experiences of women into the narrative. Longer books than this will be necessary to incorporate fully the exciting ongoing research in areas such as environmental history and the history of health and healing. Given the country's legacy of racial oppression, most professional historians in South Africa continue to be white; but we can look forward to a time when a new postapartheid generation of black scholars takes the lead in reshaping our understanding of the country's history, perhaps in unexpected ways.

South Africa
in World History

CHAPTER 1

Ancestors

On August 2, 1978, while searching for bones and tools at Lae-
toli, thirty miles south of Olduvai Gorge in northern Tanzania,
paleontologists Mary Leakey and Paul Abell discovered a series
of footprints about 3.6 million years old traceable to human ancestors.
Studying the pattern of the prints, Leakey concluded that three people,
a woman, a man, and a child, had crossed the plain. In the midst of their
walk, possibly sensing danger, the female appeared to pause and turn to
the left; she then resumed her stride. Writing in *National Geographic*,
Leakey reflected, "This motion, so intensely human, transcends time. A
remote ancestor—just as you or I—experienced a moment of doubt."[1]
Equally intriguing in attracting popular attention to the origins of
human life is the idea that all people are descended from a single ancestor whom researchers have dubbed "Lucy."

Such discoveries connect us with our remote ancestors, the earliest
human beings, known as hominids, who lived in the vast grasslands of
eastern and southern Africa about four to six million years ago. By
studying their remains in the form of bones and tools, paleontologists
and archeologists have traced both human evolution and the development of technological skills and social life in early societies. More
recently, biologists who examine the comparative genetic structure of
contemporary populations have advanced competing theories of human
origins. Although scholars in these different fields often disagree with
one another, their innovative research has revolutionized our understanding of the genesis and development of human societies.

These evolutionary patterns, which connect us to the family discovered by Mary Leakey, occurred in a vast continent with a diverse
and fluctuating physical and ecological environment. With a total land
area of some 11.7 million miles, Africa is more than three times the size
of the continental United States. In southern Africa, including present-
day South Africa, Namibia, Lesotho, Botswana, and Swaziland, high

plateaus of grassy savannah cover the central and eastern interior, with dry scrub and desert to the west and a well-watered semitropical strip along the east coast, and, in the far southwest, a four-season Mediterranean climate. Though these ecological zones seem relatively well defined, their boundaries have shifted over time in response to changing patterns of rainfall, farming, and grazing.

"Pula!" (May it rain!), a standard greeting in Lesotho, highlights the importance of rainfall to daily life and the impact of climate on economic patterns and on changes in fertility, mortality, and population growth. In most of Africa, rainfall is seasonal, with alternating wet and dry periods. Moving south from the equator, annual rainfall totals gradually diminish, with less than ten inches a year falling in the Kalahari and Namib deserts in South Africa and Namibia. Thus, farming and herding thrive during the well-watered months, leaving a six- or seven-month period with reduced levels of agricultural productivity and scarce resources for pasturing livestock. Fluctuations in precipitation from year to year make agricultural planning unpredictable. Combined with varying soil fertility, irregular rainfall causes periodic food shortages that, until recently, restricted population density in many areas. These precarious conditions promoted a belief in the value of large families and in religious ceremonies designed to encourage rainfall and celebrate abundant harvests.

The region's extensive mineral wealth has also shaped historical change. Exquisitely crafted gold jewelry found in the royal graves of early southern African states highlights the longstanding connection between precious metals and political power and the importance of gold in regional trade and patterns of consumption. Of all the gold mined throughout human history, 40 percent (more than 40,000 tons) has come from one area of South Africa. Large-scale mineral extraction is relatively recent, however, dating only to the late nineteenth century, when the European discovery of diamonds and gold in South Africa initiated a scramble for resources that dramatically reshaped the history of the entire region.

As elsewhere in the world, several major themes dominated early southern African history: increasing technological complexity and social differentiation (particularly the shift from gathering and hunting to herding and agriculture) and changing patterns of trade, intermarriage, cultural borrowing, and conflict. Despite these general trends, our knowledge of the evolution of complex societies often comes from chance discoveries. In 1924, a quarry worker was blasting limestone in an ancient cave at Taung in the northern Cape of South Africa when he

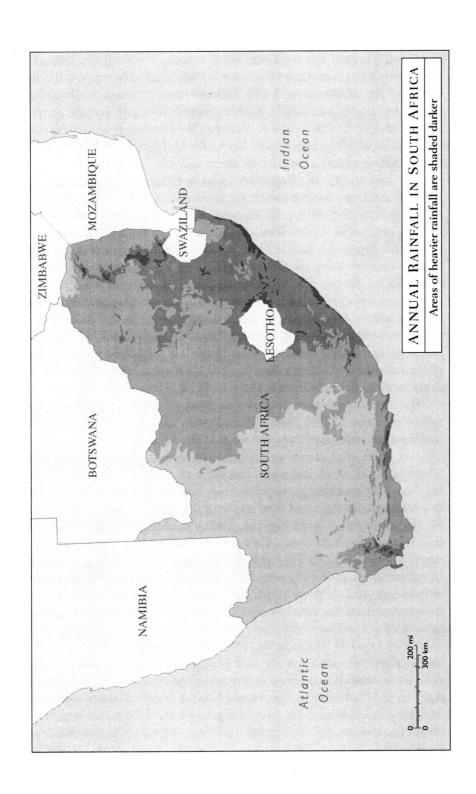

ANNUAL RAINFALL IN SOUTH AFRICA
Areas of heavier rainfall are shaded darker

ZIMBABWE

MOZAMBIQUE

BOTSWANA

NAMIBIA

SWAZILAND

LESOTHO

SOUTH AFRICA

Indian
Ocean

Atlantic
Ocean

200 mi
300 km

unearthed a mysterious skull embedded in rock. The skull was brought to Raymond Dart, an Australian-born professor of anatomy at the University of the Witwatersrand who had expressed an interest in locating prehistoric bones and fossils. Dart's conclusion—controversial at the time—that the skull belonged to a human-like creature helped to launch the theories of Mary Leakey and her husband, Louis S. B. Leakey, that human life emerged in the African savannahs.

Dry lake basins and limestone caves in remote areas of east, central, and southern Africa preserve the fossil evidence on which archeologists base their current hypothesis—that the direct ancestors of modern humans evolved in Africa between five and seven million years ago. A seven-million-year-old skull in Chad, on the southern fringes of the Sahara Desert, now provides the oldest evidence of a link between primates and humans. As the climate became cooler and drier, and large areas of open grassland replaced forests, these "hominids" gradually began to walk upright on a regular basis and to develop larger brains. Subsequent research confirmed Dart's conclusion that the Taung skull belonged to one of the first early hominids who lived about three million years ago. By about 2.5 million years ago these ancestors were making stone tools that contributed to their ability to survive on fish and scavenged animals.

During the next evolutionary era, from roughly 1.5 million years ago to between 200,000 and 100,000 years ago, our ancestors began making even more finely crafted stone tools. Known as hand axes and cleavers, these implements probably had numerous uses for digging and working wood, or as weapons. The chips or flakes produced in making them provided sharper implements for cutting and scraping. During this time, people migrated over much of the African continent, except for the most dense forest regions. Living in communities of between twenty and fifty individuals, they preferred sites near water and subsisted largely on vegetables, adding some meat from hunting. Evidence of cooperative hunting suggests that the use of language had developed and the fine finish of some hand axes points to the emergence of esthetic awareness. From this time on, evolution favored those with strong skills in communication and cooperation.

By 160,000 to 100,000 years ago anatomically modern humans, people physically similar to us, had emerged. In this evolutionary process, sometimes characterized as a progression from the "Middle Stone Age" to the "Late Stone Age," tools became finer and more complex. With these microlithic tools, people began to master the natural environment in new ways, developing more efficient methods of exploiting wild food sources. In association with these changes, language and creativity began to flourish. Indeed, new discoveries provide striking evidence that our Late Stone Age ancestors in Africa initiated the creative and symbolic thinking that distinguishes modern humans from their predecessors. The Blombos cave in South Africa, perched high above the Indian Ocean on a cliff 200 miles east of Cape Town, supports this hypothesis. While exploring this cave, Christopher Henshilwood and Judy Sealy of the South African Museum in Cape Town made discoveries that challenge the longstanding theory that such creative developments emerged more recently and originated in Europe. Artifacts more than 70,000 years old indicate that these cave dwellers were turning animal bones into sharply pointed, finely polished tools and weapon points and engraving red ochre stones with intricate geometric decorations.

Supporting these new archeological findings, genetic analysis confirms the theory that human populations originated in Africa. By studying both mitochondrial DNA in modern humans (inherited only through women) and the male or Y chromosome, biologists have drawn up a human family tree that indicates the genetic relationships between modern peoples and ancestral human populations. This analysis is possible because, unlike most genetic material, mitochondrial DNA and the Y chromosome are inherited relatively unchanged from one generation to the next. On the basis of such reconstruction, archeologists believe that by about 30,000 years ago people related to the modern foraging (hunting and gathering) peoples of southern African had spread across the eastern half of Africa, in a band stretching from South Africa to Ethiopia.

The diversity of archeological remains from this time onward provides a more complete picture of peoples' lives than is available in earlier periods. Findings at numerous sites in southern Africa show communities that crafted wooden bows and arrows and digging sticks, sewed leather bags and clothing, made strong fiber for nets, and gathered grass and soft undergrowth for bedding. The remains of plant foods suggest that some groups migrated regularly between coastal winter settlements and inland summer camps. Caves along the coast preserve the remains of fish, marine birds, seals, and whales that washed ashore as well as the bones of antelopes, tortoises, and mongooses. Grave sites from southern Africa contain tools, beads, and other personal belongings, probably indicating a belief that the dead would be able to use these objects in some kind of afterlife. Most remarkable in the region are the rock paintings and engravings, an ancient artistic tradition with varied motifs. They include human figures, sometimes armed with bows and arrows, antelope herds, and eland, associated with rain and fertility.

This rock painting from the Drakensberg Mountains is similar to thousands of paintings and engravings found throughout southern Africa. Archeologists now tend to interpret this art work as reflecting the values and beliefs of foraging communities. Eland, the largest antelope, were a frequent motif of these paintings. Their spirits were thought to influence rain, fertility, and personal and communal problems. Iziko Museums of Cape Town.

These widespread artistic remains, found all over southern Africa, provide fascinating insight into the conceptual world of early human communities. Although some of these creative works date to the nineteenth century and portray relatively straightforward scenes, such as whites firing guns at African cattle raiders, others go back to the Late Stone Age and are more difficult to interpret. Puzzled by the frequent representations of people in a bent-over position, anthropologists, observing the same posture among healers in contemporary foraging societies when in a state of trance, relate the paintings to the rich spiritual life of the hunter-gatherers.

For most of human history, people lived in hunting and gathering communities such as those that remain in remote pockets of southern Africa. They collected food from the natural environment; lived primarily on wild fruits and vegetables and the meat of wild animals and fish; and clothed themselves in skins, furs, and feathers, which in more recent times were exchanged for iron and tobacco. Wood, bone, and stone provided materials to make weapons and tools, while ostrich egg shells were perfect for storing liquids. Living in small communities (or bands) that moved frequently in search of food and water was the best strategy for survival. Members of a band shared the fruits of their gathering and hunting expeditions and met as a group to make decisions and settle disputes. Because of the limited opportunity to accumulate wealth or material goods, there were no ruling groups and anthropologists assume that relationships between women and men were considerably more equal than in subsequent stages of human existence. These societies also placed a strong emphasis on cooperation and generosity.

Descendants of ancestral foraging societies, now identified in southern Africa as San or Bushmen (Basarwa in Botswana), remained the main inhabitants of the region until about 2,500 years ago, when herding, farming, and iron technology profoundly altered social and cultural life. (The term San, also Sonqua or Soaqua, comes from the name that herding peoples gave to the foragers at the Cape, who call themselves by particular group names. It has been variously translated as "people different from ourselves" or "bandits.") With these transformations, the relationships among diverse communities became a key theme of local history, as it was throughout Africa and the rest of the world in the wake of similar developments.

Between 20,000 and 7,000 years ago people in north and northeast Africa began to add herding and cultivated plants to diets that still included fish, wild game, and foraged fruits and vegetables. Farming gradually became more widespread through the cultivation of new indigenous crops such as sorghum, millet, yams, African rice, and *teff*, an Ethiopian grain used in making unleavened bread. By gaining greater control over their food supply, farmers were able to develop a more settled way of life, paving the way for greater economic specialization and the accumulation of material possessions. Although foraging remained important to most African economies, farming has provided the primary basis for cultural and social transformation since the sixth millennium BCE.

The drying up of the formerly fertile Sahara Desert around 2500 BCE prompted the next phase in the continent's history. As large numbers of people migrated southward to find new sources of food, cereal agriculture and domestic animals moved with them. Only later, from the end of the first millennium BCE, did livestock (sheep and cattle) and farming disperse to the southern areas of the continent. By the middle of the first millennium CE, however, both cattle and sheep had spread widely in central and southern Africa, although archeological remains in South Africa and Namibia suggest that sheep herding predated the arrival of cattle from the north. Iron working also had diffused throughout the region by the first millennium CE, bringing with it profound changes in economic and social life. With this new technology, people could produce more efficient agricultural tools as well as spears, knives, ceremonial bells, and jewelry; in addition, forests could be cleared, wood worked, land cultivated, and enemies defeated with greater efficiency.

Until recently, historians and archeologists credited iron working with beginning an agricultural revolution across much of the continent. They believed that when the Sahara dried up, many of the displaced people migrated southward into West Africa. As the new technology led to overpopulation, people speaking closely related languages known as Bantu (from the root word for person, -*ntu*) spilled across central, east, and southern Africa, bringing with them knowledge of iron working, pottery, and agriculture. Armed with superior tools and weapons, they displaced or absorbed earlier foraging peoples. The basis for this hypothesis came from a comparative analysis of the hundreds of Bantu languages. However, new linguistic analysis, which dates the dispersal of Bantu-speaking peoples to a period earlier than presumed, disconnects their spread from metal smelting and agriculture. Analysis of "proto-Bantu," the reconstructed original language, now suggests that its speakers in the highlands of present-day Cameroon crafted pottery and cultivated root crops as far back as 3,000 BCE and began dispersing across the continent before the advent of metal working in west or east Africa. Contrary to earlier hypotheses, this research also suggests that Bantu languages diffused not only through migration, but in numerous ways, including trade, intermarriage, and warfare.

Distinctive ecological niches shaped the expansion of herding and agriculture into southern Africa, although irregular rainfall and difficulties storing grain encouraged interdependence between farmers and herders. In the dry regions of the west, livestock herding, supplemented by hunting and gathering, was probably established in the last few centuries BCE. In the more fertile grasslands of the Northern Province and the east coast, new Bantu-speaking arrivals began to farm between the third and seventh centuries CE, particularly in the deep fertile soils along the beds of major rivers. At the same time sheep and goats replaced fish as a main source of animal protein. Using a form of agriculture known as shifting cultivation, these farmers periodically burned the forests to open up new land for crops and grazing. As the population grew, burned-over forests became grasslands and cattle herds increased in size, helping families to survive in time of drought.

The continual search for water and pasture land makes the spread of nomadic herding easy to understand, although historians have debated whether new groups of people brought herding into southern Africa or whether some foragers gradually adopted a new way of life. Whatever their origins, both groups speak closely related languages with distinctive click sounds, now known as Khoisan, and the boundaries between them were extremely fluid. In times of disease or drought, herders who lost their cattle might fall back on foraging until they could rebuild their stock through theft or by working as clients for wealthier men. But herders expressed their sense of distinctiveness by calling themselves Khoekhoe (or Khoikhoi), meaning the "real people" or "real men."

Unlike their more egalitarian foraging neighbors, herders formed communities in which wealth in livestock—including fat-tailed sheep (a breed well suited to arid dry conditions), long-horned cattle, and oxen—became the primary measure of status and prestige. Although cattle could not be bought and sold, owners of large herds (sometimes numbering in the thousands) could acquire power by lending cows to other men, who then became their clients. Both men and women rode oxen, used as pack animals, and, unusual for southern Africa, women milked cattle and retained control over the cows they received as bride-wealth gifts from their husbands' families. While the ecological environment defined daily life through the continual need to find pasture and water for livestock, and milk was the dietary staple, people also hunted, fished, and collected honey along with wild roots and berries as did their foraging neighbors.

Religious life revolved around ceremonies to promote rainfall, a necessity in a drought-prone environment, and on beliefs in such spiritual figures as Tsui-‖Goab, a creator or founding ancestor and guardian of health, and ‖Gaunab, believed to cause sickness and death. (The double lines stand for a click sound.) Commenting on the values of these communities, Olfert Dapper, a Dutch geographic writer who published a detailed and comprehensive study of contemporary knowledge about southern Africa in 1668, wrote: "In generosity and loyalty to those nearest them, they appear to shame the Dutch. For instance, if one of them has anything he will willingly share it with another; no matter how small it may be, they will always endeavour to share and divide it amongst themselves in a brotherly manner."[2]

Although herders moved frequently in search of pasture and water, in contrast to gatherers and hunters they remained in one place long enough for established villages to develop and for some families to emerge as hereditary leaders. These local elites judged disputes (along with the wealthiest stock-owners) and decided when and where the group should seek new pasture lands. M. K. H. Lichtenstein, a naturalist and traveler at the Cape, wrote in 1806 of the limited power of the chief, observing that "His authority is exceedingly circumscribed, and no one considers himself as wholly bound to yield obedience to him; neither does he himself ever pretend to command them."[3] People lived in round huts, with frames of green branches planted into the ground, bent over, and tied together. These houses, covered simply with reed mats, could be easily moved. A brush fence surrounding each community enclosed cattle at night. Villages, often numbering more than 100 people, grouped together in larger networks of up to several thousand people who shared food and intermarried. Related communities reinforced their relationships with each other by having newly married men live with their wives' families until the first child was born. With population density low, there was little competition for pasture land. When Dutch newcomers arrived at the tip of southern Africa in the seventeenth century, these herding communities bore the brunt of their intrusion.

Because they moved so frequently, dense archeological remains of herding communities are scarce. The situation is different for cultivators, who lived a more sedentary life. In the mid-1990s, archeologists working in the northeastern corner of South Africa, on the border between South Africa, Zimbabwe, and Mozambique, began to excavate a stone wall and royal grave site, one of more than five hundred hilltop stone remains scattered along the Limpopo River basin. Their discoveries along these fertile riverbeds revealed relics of southern Africa's earliest centralized states, whose leaders based their power and wealth on international Indian Ocean trading networks that connected them with the Middle East and India. Ruling from imposing dry-stone enclosures, these kings claimed large numbers of followers and extensive cattle herds. The royal site of Mapungubwe and the neighboring village of K2 were the center of a thriving kingdom between 1000 and 1300 CE whose remains include gold jewelry, iron fragments, glass beads, crafted ivory, and bone tools. The remnants of spinning wheels point to a local cotton weaving industry, and among the most striking discoveries were a rhinoceros and a scepter and bowl made of gold sheet tacked onto a wooden carving. Archeologists at the later site of Thulamela ("place of birth," c. 1200–1600) found a royal grave decorated with gold and another body, believed to be a ruler's wife. She was buried with her hands folded below her chin—a pose of respect among the area's contemporary inhabitants. These states, perched on the high sandstone cliffs

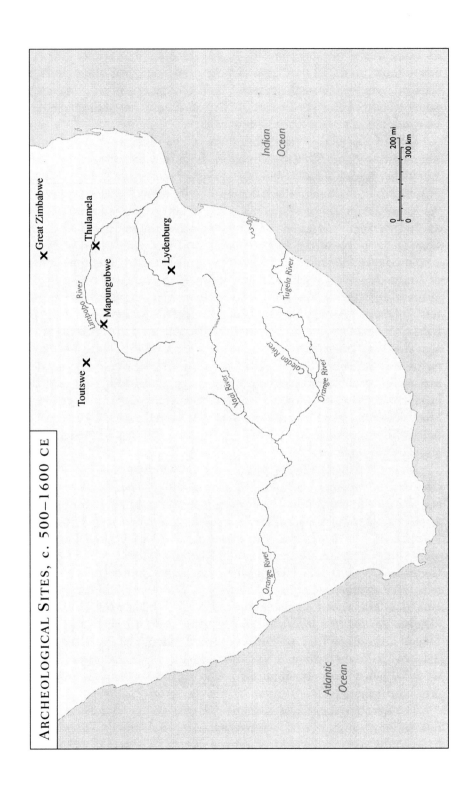

ARCHEOLOGICAL SITES, c. 500–1600 CE

Great Zimbabwe

Thulamela

Lydenburg

Mapungubwe

Toutswe

Limpopo River

Vaal River

Caledon River

Orange River

Tugela River

Orange River

Indian Ocean

Atlantic Ocean

200 mi

300 km

towering above the Limpopo River, also include Toutswe, c. 700 CE, one of more than 250 sites from this early period. When Mapungubwe declined, whether through environmental change or shifts in trade, the center of power flowed eastward to Thulamela and north to the better-known kingdom of the Great Zimbabwe.

One of the most vivid descriptions of the societies that followed Mapungubwe and Thulamela comes from the autobiography that nationalist leader Nelson Mandela smuggled out of his Robben Island prison cell. In the book he recalled his childhood in the rural Transkei, "a beautiful country of rolling hills, fertile valleys, and a thousand rivers and streams"[4] where his father was a government-appointed chief. Though he writes of the early twentieth century, many aspects of his account evoke life among his Xhosa ancestors (and other communities of Bantu-speaking farmers and herders) in earlier times. Families lived in beehive-shaped houses with mud walls in which a peaked, thatched roof balanced on a central wooden pole. Mandela's mother had three huts, one used for cooking, another for sleeping, and the third for storage. Cooking either outdoors or in the center of the house, she prepared food on an open fire in a three-legged iron pot. The dietary staple, maize, was ground and made into a porridge eaten with sour milk or beans. As a young boy expected to herd sheep and calves, he discovered "the almost mystical attachment that the Xhosa have for cattle, not only as a source of food and wealth, but as a blessing from God and a source of happiness."[5]

Mandela depicts a highly stratified society in which everyone's status was clearly defined, including women and men, chiefs and commoners, and elders and youth. Those considered close family encompassed a wide range of relatives. "I hardly recall any occasion as a child when I was alone," he wrote. "In African culture, the sons and daughters of one's aunts or uncles are considered brothers and sisters, not cousins."[6] Community values, which emphasized cattle and honoring one's ancestors, were communicated in part through a rich tradition of storytelling, and Mandela thrived on the legends and fables his mother recounted. He also learned to appreciate the importance of ancestral veneration. "If you dishonored your ancestors in some fashion," he explained, "the only way to atone for that lapse was to consult with a traditional healer or tribal elder, who communicated with the ancestors and conveyed profound apologies."[7]

The autobiography also recounts the process that led Mandela to full manhood and political involvement. After his father's death, when he was nine years old, Mandela went to live with the acting paramount chief of the Thembu, a Xhosa clan. Living at the royal court, he was immersed in preparation for a leadership role among his people. He became fascinated with the process of government, attending open meetings where men gathered to discuss drought or cattle and settle disputes, and where poets recited eulogies to rulers, both ancient and modern, and satirized current power holders. When Mandela was sixteen years old he experienced the painful circumcision ceremony that transformed youth into men—receiving a new name and undergoing a period of seclusion during which he was painted with white ochre to symbolize purity—a time he described as "a kind of spiritual preparation for the trials of manhood."[8] Although the trials Mandela would face were far different from those of his distant ancestors, his rural upbringing reflected many aspects of life in earlier times.

During the second millennium CE, societies such as the Xhosa, which survived by combining agriculture with herding and hunting, became well established throughout the northern, central, and eastern parts of present-day South Africa. People spoke Bantu languages closely related to those elsewhere in Africa; but the click sounds in some languages as well as borrowed words for sheep, ram, cattle, ox, and sour milk affirmed their ties with neighboring Khoisan speakers. With ample land available, these farmers continued to practice shifting cultivation, moving to new areas when population increases exhausted the soil, and burning the forests to claim the newly fertile fields for farming and pasture. One of the earliest external descriptions of these communities, which emphasizes their dependence on cattle keeping and women's labor, came from the survivors of a Portuguese ship that went aground on the east coast in 1635. They reported of the local people: "There are rich and poor among them, but this is according to the number of their cattle. . . . The kings have four, five, and seven wives. The women do all the work, planting and tilling the earth with sticks to prepare it for their grain. . . . Cows are what they chiefly value: these are very fine and the tamest cattle I have ever seen in any country. In the milk season they live chiefly upon it, making curds and turning it sour, which was little to our taste. . . . The women bring no dowry in marriage, on the contrary the husband pays the bride's father with cattle."[9]

This description accurately captures many aspects of these mixed-farming communities in which family members had to work together to sustain a stable food supply. Their main crop was sorghum (a drought-resistant grain), supplemented by beans, pumpkins, calabashes, and melons. By the seventeenth century, maize and tobacco had arrived from the Americas via Portuguese trading networks. Women planted, hoed, weeded, and harvested the crops, while men took responsibility for heavy tasks such as clearing the fields and building huts. Despite the key role women played in farming, older men had the authority to allocate land to each family and, with the exception of unusually powerful women, men alone could own cattle. As in earlier times, by combining cultivation with raising cattle, sheep, and goats, families could ensure subsistence in areas in which rainfall was unpredictable. Hunting also supplemented the food supply, producing skins for clothing and, particularly from the seventeenth century onward, ivory that might be traded at the coast. Regular trade with neighboring areas ensured that everyone had essential goods such as iron and salt. Copper ornaments, more of a luxury, were also widespread.

Cattle not only were crucial to economic survival and social organization, as they were for the Khoekhoe, but were also primary symbols of wealth and power. Cattle owners with large herds might build up personal networks by lending cows to poorer men. Gifts of cattle also established powerful ties among families when children married. By exchanging cows (or, in some areas, iron hoes) for wives in bridewealth, gifts presented by the man's family to that of the woman, men rich in livestock could marry more than one woman, thereby acquiring the labor to cultivate larger plots of land. Wives and children added to a family's wealth and prestige. As a gift that generally had to be returned in case of divorce, bridewealth stabilized marriage. Since a married woman and her children lived with her husband's family, these exchanges also compensated the woman's family for the loss of an economically active member.

In a society where everyone's position was clearly defined, fathers and husbands had considerable control over daughters and wives, and the idea that older members of the group (women and men) should command respect from the young permeated all social relationships: between rulers and family heads, patrons and clients, husbands and wives, and parents and children. These principles also influenced relationships among women. Thus, mothers-in-law held authority over wives, as did older over younger co-wives. One Xhosa woman, healer and storyteller Nongenile Masithathu Zenani, described her behavior when she first married: "Even in the way that I walked, I showed deference. I went about that homestead [of her husband's family] very carefully, . . . being very submissive to my in-laws. . . . I continued to act like that until I began to sense that I was pregnant, that I would soon give birth to a child."[10]

In communities in which well-being depended on agricultural abundance, the fertility of both women and the land was central to religion

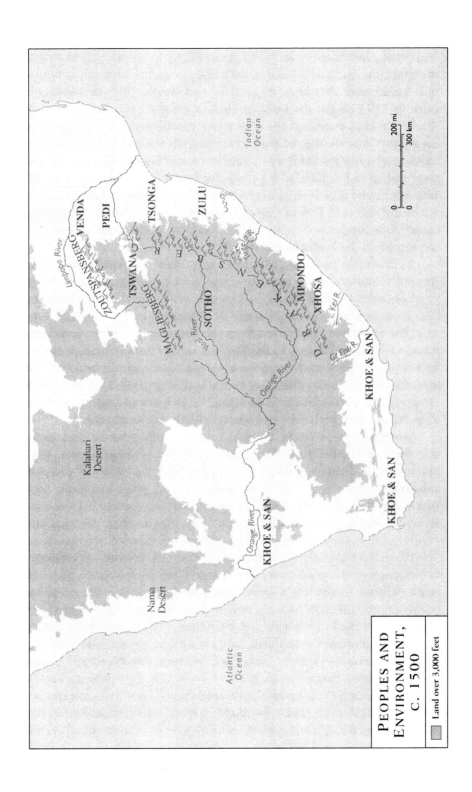

Indian Ocean

200 mi
300 km

VENDA
PEDI
TSONGA
ZULU
ZOUTPANSBERG
Limpopo River
TSWANA
MAGLIESBERG
SOTHO
MPONDO
XHOSA
Kei R.
Gt Fish R.
Vaal River
Orange River
KHOE & SAN

Kalahari Desert

KHOE & SAN

Nama Desert

Orange River
KHOE & SAN

KHOE & SAN

Atlantic Ocean

PEOPLES AND
ENVIRONMENT,
C. 1500

Land over 3,000 feet

and ritual. Ceremonies marked stages in the agricultural cycle as well as the rites of passage in an individual's life, from birth through initiation into adulthood, marriage, childbirth, and death. Naboth Mokgatle, born in 1911 in the Rustenburg District (in the area then known as the Transvaal), described the customary marriage process in his autobiography: "At the age of twelve or thirteen, the girl was told by her mother who her husband was going to be and who her parents-in-law were going to be. Similarly, before the boy left for circumcision, his father told him whose daughter he was going to marry and the name of his future wife. . . . Before they got married, they . . . were not allowed to be alone, or given time to ask one another whether they knew they were going to be husband and wife."[11]

As Mandela observed, the most important spiritual forces were recently deceased lineage ancestors, who were commemorated with regular observances. Men who were family heads guided these ceremonies, which emphasized the importance of descent through the male line, as in the following description from the Sotho area. "When a Mosuto dreams of his dead father, he thinks it is a supernatural visitation caused by his own neglect; and, upon the diviner's advice, an ox or a sheep of a certain colour is sacrificed . . . and prayer is offered: 'Oh, let us now sleep in peace, and trouble us no more.'"[12] In areas of centralized kingship, royal dead, both men and women, were also venerated.

Spiritual power could be exercised in both positive and negative ways, particularly in relation to illness and healing. Women were prominent as diviners, who could explain the complexities of personal relationships in the present and future, and as spirit mediums, who communicated with deities and with shades of the deceased. They were trusted advisors to those who sought their assistance in personal and community matters. Zulu diviners, almost all married women, were identified through a mysterious illness that an experienced practitioner attributed to spirit possession. Xhosa storyteller Mrs. Zenani, who had felt a vocation to become a doctor when she got married, described her persistent nervousness, anxiety, and intense chest pain after four of her children had died. Following her treatment, "The pains in my chest ended, my anxieties were calmed"; she then began to treat other patients until the doctor instructed: "Well, it's about time that she should go and set up her own practice, . . . because she's now got quite a clientele here."[13] Working for the good of the community, these religious specialists were called on to ensure harmony in both individual and collective relationships. But spiritual power could also be used to cause harm, and most people saw witchcraft as a possible explanation of misfortune, believing that some individuals had the power to damage other people as well as their crops and livestock.

Apart from the early kingdoms that flourished in the Limpopo River Valley, until the seventeenth century most inhabitants of southern Africa lived in relatively small-scale communities organized around homesteads, districts that incorporated several extended families, and small states or chiefdoms of no more than 1,000 people. Subordinate to the official above him, the head of each group had his own court, cattle enclosure, and settlement areas. Leadership was hereditary through the male line and abundant farm land enabled discontented or ambitious individuals to found their own states, which were identified by individual ancestral names. Based on language similarities, historians have identified two main groups: Nguni (most prominently the present-day Xhosa and Zulu along the east coast) and Sotho (now Sotho and Tswana, occupying the center and north of the region). Two smaller groups included the Venda, in the far north, and the Tsonga along the northern coast.

From c. 1600 onward, increasing external trade, growing centralization of political power, and extensive population movement destabilized these political and economic patterns. As trade expanded, mainly with Portuguese settlements on the east coast, chiefs began to exploit and extend the areas under their control to supply products for export. Among the Sotho-speaking peoples and the Venda, these rulers were often women. The development of larger states with intensified demands for labor and tribute prompted major migrations as people sought better grazing land for their cattle and land that could produce ivory, furs, and metals for trade. The importance of trade notwithstanding, oral traditions suggest that disputes over succession or competition for cattle and wives remained more important sources of conflict than competition for tribute in trade goods. In the area north of the Vaal River (and particularly on the Waterberg plateau roughly 100 miles north of present-day Johannesburg), the most striking development was the emergence of hill-top defensive settlements among Sotho/Tswana/Pedi-speaking groups that protected them from raiders known as Ndebele, the Sotho name for Nguni speakers.

By the eighteenth and nineteenth centuries, the Tswana states had diverged decisively from others in the region, developing large capital towns of anywhere from 10,000 to 25,000 inhabitants. Probably a result of the introduction of maize (which could yield three times the harvest of sorghum and millets), population growth contributed to larger, more centralized kingdoms. One means of expansion was for rulers wealthy in cattle to offer lavish bridewealth gifts, thus expanding their networks of dependents and the territory over which they ruled. Since these states did not practice primogeniture, increasing numbers of wives and children meant growing competition for succession in addition to intensified disputes over bridewealth. By the early nineteenth century, this growing conflict set the stage for more violent and intense warfare.

A rich heritage of oral literature, including poetry, stories, and historical narratives, transmitted the culture and values of these societies. Poetry might celebrate the bravery of distinguished warriors or political leaders, lament the downtrodden situation of women in the homes of their mothers-in-law, or recount catastrophic historic events. In one poem collected in Lesotho in 1842, women bemoaned the aftermath of war.

> Alas! Are they really gone?
> Are we abandoned indeed?
> But where have they gone
> That they cannot come back?[14]

Zulu praise poems, called *izibongo*, which celebrate the personality and achievements of both rulers and ordinary people, illustrate the wide range of oral literature. Poetry honoring powerful men emphasized masculine warlike values, extolling physical courage and endurance. These poems repeated images such as the blood-spattered shield or assegai (spear) or rivers flowing with blood. Part of a poem recited for Dingiswayo, a late eighteenth- and early nineteenth-century ruler, boasts of his military prowess:

> Trail Blazer like the vulture along the path; he is red; with the blood
>   of men.
> Inventor; overcoming other chiefs; through his fresh devising.[15]

Zulu men's private poems, performed at weddings and coming of age celebrations, use this heroic medium to honor ordinary people.

Women's poetry, performed in more private spaces open only to other women, chronicled relations with co-wives and mothers-in-law, courtship, and marital mistreatment; but at times these recitations also celebrated women's strength and resilience. One powerful poem recited by MaJele, the junior third wife of a former chief, memorialized her fierce and passionate life before marriage:

> I am she who cuts across the game reserve
> That no girl crosses.
> I am the boldest of the bold, outfacer of wizards.

Obstinate perseverer,
The nation swore at me and ate their words,
She cold shoulders kings and despises mere commoners.[16]

Alongside this expressive oral culture, other arts also flourished, from San rock paintings to sculpture, pottery, basketry, and beadwork. The seven terra cotta heads found at Lydenburg in the eastern Transvaal (now Mpumalanga) dated to 500–700 CE are particularly striking. Ranging in size from 12 to 20 inches, these heads featured incised decorations similar to those on the pottery found at the site; the two largest may have been used as ceremonial masks. Over a longer period of time, men carved elaborate wooden headrests, which were said to establish communication with ancestral spirits, and made baskets decorated with

This sculpture was one of seven terra cotta heads dated to 500–700 CE found at Lydenburg in the eastern Transvaal (now Mpumalanga). The heads, which range in size from 12 to 20 inches, are the earliest known sculptures found in southern Africa. Their incised decorations are similar to those on the pottery found at the site. While their meaning is not certain, the sculptures may have been used in initiation rituals, the two largest possibly as ceremonial masks. Iziko Museums of Cape Town.

This Zulu headrest from Pietermaritzburg in KwaZulu-Natal province is dated to ca. 1900. Such wooden sculptures probably were used as stools during the day and, at night, as headrests that mediated communication with the ancestors through sleep and dreams. Photograph by Franko Khoury. National Museum of African Art, Smithsonian Institution.

bold geometric patterns; women crafted clay pots with intricate decorations. Tsonga, Swazi, and Lobedu people in the northeastern corner of South Africa produced carved human figures associated with initiation societies and elaborate beadwork jewelry and clothing that distinguished people of different ages and rank. In Zulu society, small beaded squares facilitated communication between young women and their male friends, with different colors and designs communicating coded messages. A triangle with the apex pointing up, for example, signified an unmarried woman, while the color black could indicate sadness as well as marriage.

Beginning in the 1590s, when Dutch and English sailors arrived on the coast, this complex world would begin to face new challenges. Coming from European countries that were aggressively acquiring new colonial outposts, these sailors were following the path of Portuguese traders, already settled in Mozambique. Although people of different languages and cultures had interacted intensively over land for thousands of years, apart from the indirect effects of Indian Ocean trade, the region had remained relatively isolated from external contact by sea. The ancestors of Mandela and MaJele could not have known that over time, the appearance of these strangers would dramatically transform the life they knew.

CHAPTER 2

Bitter Almond Hedges: Colonization, Servitude, and Slavery

In December 1651 the Dutch East India Company (VOC) appointed the merchant Jan Van Riebeeck to establish and command a permanent settlement on the southern tip of Africa. After sailing for nearly four months, he arrived at the Cape of Good Hope on April 6, 1652 with his wife and son, eighty-two men, and seven women. While concerned primarily with the valuable spices from its colonial outpost at Batavia in the East Indies, the Company had to supply sailors with fresh fruits and vegetables midway through the long journey from the Netherlands to keep them from dying of scurvy. In the interests of trade, the new commander was instructed to keep the peace with the area's indigenous population.

Soon after Van Riebeeck arrived, a twelve-year-old Khoekhoe girl named Krotoa came to live with his family. Initially a servant, once she had learned to speak Dutch fluently she became a valued interpreter between the two cultures. Renamed Eva, she provided Van Riebeeck with valuable inside information about Khoekhoe politics and plans, contributing to the cross-cultural communication that enabled the Dutch to acquire livestock in exchange for tobacco, copper, beads, and drink.

This period of peaceful exchange lasted only briefly. As conflicts escalated over runaway slaves and Dutch confiscation of cattle and land, Eva found herself in the middle of these disputes. To salvage her position, she tried to encourage alliances and trade between the colonial intruders and local rulers, in one case persuading the Dutch to send violinists and a clown to entertain a potential ally. When Eva married a Danish physician, Pieter van Meerhof, who became a high-ranking soldier in the Dutch East India Company, they sought together to expand Dutch trade with outlying areas. But van Meerhof's death on an expedition

Dutch engraving presenting an image of peaceful trade between the Khoekhoe and European sailors in the seventeenth century. From the 1590s onward, Dutch and British sailors en route to Asia made regular stops at Table Bay. Their exchanges of iron, copper, and tobacco for Khoekhoe sheep and cattle were often more violent than this picture suggests. Museum Africa, Johannesburg.

to Mauritius in 1667, following Van Riebeeck's transfer to Malacca in the East Indies five years earlier, intensified Eva's ambivalent position as an indigenous woman trying to live in European society. Despite her conversion to Christianity and her linguistic fluency, her two protectors, Van Riebeeck and Pieter, were gone. From then on, the Dutch commanders accused Eva of drunkenness, prostitution, and abandoning her three children; on several occasions they imprisoned her on Robben Island, seven and a half miles from Cape Town. Cold and windswept, with a dangerous rocky coastline that caused frequent shipwrecks over the years, the island would later house South Africa's most famous political prisoners. There Eva died a lonely death in 1674.

The tragic ending of Eva's life reflects the divisions of the early colonial era—a period of initial cordiality, followed by constantly shifting alliances, all in the context of continually widening discord between the Dutch and local societies. Within another century, stripped of livestock and grazing land and ravaged by disease, Khoekhoe society itself would be destroyed. Symbolic of these divisions, during the 1660s the Dutch East India Company planted a bitter almond hedge around its settlement in Cape Town. The "enormous intertwined branches" of these trees and "a tendency to grow horizontally as much as vertically"[1] provided an effective boundary between the colonists and the Cape's indigenous people.

The Dutch were not the first Europeans to round the Cape of Good Hope. Their settlement followed 164 years of sporadic contact between Europeans and various Khoekhoe and San groups near the coast. During the seventeenth century, when the Netherlands replaced Portugal as Europe's strongest maritime nation, Dutch and British ships sailing to Asia began to use the Cape as a convenient stopping point. Sailors took in cattle and sheep from those Khoekhoe willing to trade with them and offered iron, copper, and tobacco in exchange. Though mutual suspicion was high and violence was frequent, the trade became important to both sides, allowing Europeans to resupply their ships and giving the Khoekhoe a steady supply of iron that made their spears more deadly. Because the primary interest of the trading companies lay in the spice-rich possessions of the Indies, the Khoe had no reason to question their assumption that Europeans were temporary sojourners on their shores.

When the Dutch arrived, foraging and herding societies were closely linked through trade and intermarriage. Eva's father came from a group of hunter-gatherers who lived by collecting shellfish; her mother's family were pastoralists. The Dutch described the herders as swift runners who kept large numbers of oxen and fat-tailed sheep. They dressed in skins and decorated themselves with beads and ornaments of copper, iron, ivory, and brass; some inhabited makeshift housing that could be moved with ease, whereas others lived in villages with houses laid out in a circle. Seventeenth-century Dutch geographic writer Olfert Dapper, who painstakingly compiled contemporary existing knowledge of Africa, reflected the common derogatory judgment of his contemporaries when he described the people now known as Khoekhoe: "All the Kafirs or Hottentots are people bereft of all science and literature, very uncouth, and in intellect more like beasts than men."[2] Yet Dapper also reported contradictions in these attitudes and stated that many observers had commented favorably on their "liberality and hospitality"[3] and noted that as "dull-witted and coarse as these people are" when asked why they were stealing European cattle "they replied that they were doing so for no other reason than to avenge the suffering and injustice they had experienced at our taking away and sowing their lands."[4]

HOE ZY DE VISSCHEN VANGEN.

Men fishing with spears in the early eighteenth century. The drawing was done by Peter Kolb, a German astronomer and mathematician who lived at the Cape between 1705 and 1713 and wrote a book about his experiences three years after returning to Germany. One of the book's three sections discussed the social and cultural life of the people he called "Hottentots" or "Bosjesmen." National Library of South Africa.

Many aspects of indigenous societies made them vulnerable to the European invaders. Accustomed to extensive long-distance trade in cattle, iron, and copper, some Khoekhoe at first welcomed the opportunity to acquire goods from a new partner. Because men without cattle regularly worked for wealthier patrons, some men also willingly accepted employment from Europeans. When tensions arose, however, they found it difficult to protect their communities. Relatively small, fluid political units and unstable leadership made them less able than more centralized African communities to challenge European incursions successfully over a long period. Furthermore, they had no permanent armies or military leaders, and most wars were over in a day since Khoekhoe commanders were more concerned with capturing cattle than with killing their enemies. Their favored weapons—assegais (spears) and walking sticks—were no match for Dutch firepower. When a group of Khoekhoe, under the leadership of Eva's rival interpreter, Doman, attacked the colonists in 1659, they succeeded in destroying European farms and stealing most of their sheep and cattle. But they were unable to keep their fragile coalition together. Nonetheless, one aspect of Khoekhoe military strategy was effective against the Dutch—the practice of making massive, sudden attacks on an enemy's herds and then vanishing into the bush. Such guerrilla tactics served them well against greater military power, as they would for countless other African protagonists against Europeans in the coming years.

Despite his initial interest in peaceful relations with the Khoekhoe, Van Riebeeck enacted several policy changes that would have devastating effects, intensifying the collision course between Europeans and the region's indigenous inhabitants. In 1657 some of the "servants" (employees) of the Dutch East India Company were released from their contracts so that they might become free settlers; two years later, to address the labor shortage, slaves began to be imported. Van Riebeeck believed that by allowing settlers to plant food crops and raise their own livestock the fledgling colony would become more self-sufficient. But as Europeans seized land as private property and expanded their cultivated fields, they encroached on local supplies of pasture land and water. Although several Khoe groups formed a coalition in the late 1650s to try to stop this aggressive expansion, their efforts failed. Within a decade, the Khoekhoe who lived closest to the Cape Peninsula were becoming less threatening to the Dutch as their society began to crumble under foreign confiscation of their land and resources.

Dutch success against the Khoekhoe resulted not only from the seizure of land, but also from deliberate efforts to exacerbate conflict

CABO DE GOEDE HOOP.

MuseuMAfricA, Johannesburg. B247

*Khoekhoe village near Table Bay (1706), drawn by Abraham Bogaert, a physician
with the Dutch East India Company who stopped at Table Bay in 1702 and 1706.
The houses pictured here were made from a frame of green branches bent over
and covered with reed mats. The mats could be rolled up and moved easily once
grazing was depleted in one area.* Museum Africa, Johannesburg.

among Khoe groups by regularly interfering in their disputes. Local
leaders fed into this process by seeking European backing against longtime rivals. By the mid-1670s, the Dutch East India Company ended
earlier policies of hospitality toward visiting Khoekhoe dignitaries, and
suspected criminals might be lashed and shipped in chains to Robben
Island. After war broke out in 1673 with Gonnema, the chief of the
Cochoqua group, over alleged attacks on Europeans, the victorious
Dutch seized thousands of sheep and cattle, which they then redistrib-
uted to white settlers and their Khoekhoe allies. Living just to the north
of Cape Town, the Cochoqua were particularly vulnerable to conflict
with the newcomers. Several years later, when a new Dutch governor
sought to restore peace, Gonnema promised to present tribute of thirty
cattle a year to the Dutch East India Company, thereby acknowledging
their presence, if not their legitimacy, at the Cape. This humiliating settlement further reduced the independence of Khoe leaders, tying them
more closely to the Dutch. By the eighteenth century new chiefs, whom
the Dutch now called "captains," had lost their autonomy entirely;
installed by the Dutch governor, they were dependent on the Company
for any authority they retained.

During the first centuries of Dutch rule, neither cooperation nor resistance was able to stem the tide of foreign commercial and military power or to prevent the decimation of Khoekhoe herds, which had formed the basis of their livelihood. Apart from the milk, meat, and clothing lost when livestock was used for trade rather than for sustenance, white frontier farmers consistently stole cattle and sheep from their indigenous neighbors, raising the potential for devastating military conflict between Khoe communities and the Dutch. Whereas in the early years of Dutch settlement, Khoekhoe had been reluctant to work for colonists, by the 1690s, with much of their livestock confiscated, some of them were forced to become poorly paid laborers on frontier farms, supplementing the work performed by slaves. By the time of the first smallpox epidemic in 1713, the Dutch settlers regarded the loss of population not as a gift from God, as did the New England Puritans in North America, but as an unfortunate assault on their workforce.

Although the white population remained small during the seventeenth and early eighteenth century (only about two thousand free settlers, 350 of them women, by 1717), new Europeans continued to arrive, fueling the frontier expansion that threatened indigenous communities farther from the Cape Colony. French Huguenots fleeing persecution in 1685 after the revocation of the Edict of Nantes (which had granted Protestants religious and civil rights) established new wine-growing communities outside Cape Town. Required to use Dutch in schools, churches, and for any official communication, they quickly assimilated into the local white population. These French Protestants joined a stream of Dutch and German sailors and soldiers working for the Dutch East India Company, hunters and explorers, escaped slaves, indentured Company servants (known as knechts), and many others fleeing confinement, regulation, taxes, or persecution in Europe. Despite its best efforts at control, the Company never succeeded in regulating this new incursion. As the number of European settlers increased, so did conflicts with the Khoekhoe over land and livestock. Angered when Khoe herders encroached on cultivated land, settlers often raided local livestock, at times confiscating thousands of sheep and cattle.

As these settlers spread out from Cape Town, they transformed the landscape in numerous ways. Unlike the Khoekhoe and the San, they claimed clearly marked plots of land as private property, despite the original status of their holdings as "loan farms" from the VOC. In these sparsely populated regions, their large multigenerational families kept people connected with each other and helped them to maintain ties with

Cape Town and its immediate hinterland. These kin networks were sustained in part through marriages of close cousins and unions of multiple siblings to each other, both strategies that kept property within the extended family. The Dutch Reformed Church further strengthened their sense of shared identity and community, reinforced in each household through regular worship led by the family patriarch. And, despite class divisions among the settlers, frontier life was fluid enough to encourage social mobility, whether through hard work or well-planned marriage alliances.

On February 13, 1713, a fleet of ships whose passengers were infected with smallpox dropped anchor at Table Bay. Their tainted clothes were among the items taken for washing at the Company's slave lodge. By April, local slaves had developed large, infectious blisters and six to eight slaves were dying each day. Within a month, the disease had spread to whites, who were often buried without coffins because there was not time to bring sufficient wood into town to build them. But the population struck hardest was the Khoekhoe, whose immunity to the disease was far lower than that of either whites or slaves. One visitor to the Cape reported of the Khoe: "They lay everywhere on the roads . . . cursing at the Dutchmen, who they said had bewitched them."[5] Smallpox remained endemic in southern Africa for another century, with two more epidemics in 1755 and 1767.

For the Khoekhoe in the Western Cape, the combination of war, impoverishment, and disease was devastating, killing large numbers of people and destroying what remained of community life. During the eighteenth century, Khoekhoe social life disintegrated rapidly and, despite their theoretical freedom, those who remained were treated more and more like slaves. In 1775 a new law allowed farmers to indenture the children of Khoekhoe women and male slaves until the age of twenty-five years. As their own society eroded, the Khoe became a lower caste in white society, ranking below slaves in the eyes of Europeans. Prejudice against them established barriers to better jobs, intermarriage, religious conversion, or social acceptance. Although the Company forbade the enslavement of the Khoe, Europeans regarded them with utter disdain, pointing to the tragic life of Eva to suggest that the Khoekhoe would never successfully absorb European culture.

Nonetheless, despite European scorn, there was more cultural exchange than the colonists were willing to acknowledge. The Khoe were acquiring a taste for tobacco, alcohol, and some European food, and beginning to speak simplified forms of Dutch and Portuguese (learned from slaves). Unable to change the arid climate, Europeans, like the indigenous population, were forced to supplement herding with hunting and to move their livestock in search of water. And, while many settler families acquired more furniture, glassware, books, and other trappings of respectable domesticity during the course of the eighteenth century, at first most of the newcomers led austere lives, preferring (like the Khoe) to keep their wealth in livestock and to invest any surplus in agricultural tools.

In the pastoral areas farthest from the colony, some European settlers (who became known as *trekboers*, seminomadic farmers) also grew increasingly like the Khoekhoe in their social and cultural practices. They not only acquired large herds of cattle and sheep, which became a measure of wealth, but exchanged livestock to mark births and marriages, and lent sheep and cattle to poorer men who became their dependents. Like the Khoekhoe, they often built thatched-roofed houses of clay and reed and burned over the land to enhance its fertility. The poverty that many European visitors found in these areas led them to observe with alarm that the division between settlers and "natives" was disappearing. Indeed, by the late eighteenth century nearly half of frontier residents probably lived on the edge of survival.

The destruction of San communities paralleled that of the Khoekhoe. Pushed out of their customary areas as the European frontier expanded, these foraging groups faced loss of the land they had relied on for gathering and hunting; as European farmers destroyed their land and slaughtered the game critical to their food supply, the size of bands increased and new forms of defense were required. As a result, beginning in 1738 there was a wave of interconnected attacks on colonists. The raids and reprisals of European commandos (militia units), now known as the "Bushman War" of 1739, represented a turning point. This conflict, and the continuing "Bushman Wars" that began in 1770, led to commandos capturing many San, particularly women and children, and distributing them among themselves after expeditions. Although, like the Khoekhoe, they remained technically free, many of these captives and their children were indentured for long periods of time. By virtually enslaving people within their home areas, Europeans were constructing a system that encouraged flight and desertion; the brutal punishments given to recaptured runaways prompted violent retaliatory attacks on employers. As a result of these conflicts, settlers came to perceive the San as vermin who could be kept under control only by violence. The British traveler John Barrow wrote in 1797: "I myself have heard one of the humane colonists boast of having destroyed with his own hands near three hundred of these unfortunate wretches."[6]

On the night of March 12, 1736, five thatched-roof houses burned to the ground when a fire ignited a tannery in Cape Town. This blaze, which came at the end of a parched summer, might have destroyed the entire city without swift action to protect nearby properties. Investigation of suspected arson led Cape authorities to a band of runaway slaves living at Hanglip on the nearby coast under the leadership of Leander Bugis, whose name indicated his East Indian origins. Protected by a rocky shore line and rugged mountain terrain, some fifty people found refuge in this community of maroons (escaped slaves) over a period of more than ten years, though it probably sustained no more than ten people at any given time. The fugitives lived on fish, mussels, and other seafood but required regular forays into Cape Town to gather additional provisions, sufficient clothing for the chilly Cape winters, and supplies of lead, powder, and flints for their guns. To obtain other supplies and sheep, they attacked neighboring farms. Most of the runaways—including at least eight women—were in their twenties when they escaped; of those whose origins were known, almost all had arrived in South Africa as captives. The fate of those who were recaptured illustrates the brutality of the system from which the maroons had fled. Two men accused of murder were condemned to death, either by hanging or being broken on a cross. Others suffered flogging and branding before being returned to their masters.

After the fire of March 1735, the authorities sent out a commando unit against the Hanglip survivors but failed to arrest anyone. In September a second raid was more successful, capturing five members of the group. Among those who escaped, Perra von Malabar wandered on Table Mountain for ten days and then, desperately hungry, returned to his master. Leander Bugis also fled; whether he escaped or was shot to death is not clear. Though no other runaways were captured during the raid, Hanglip's complex network of caves remained a safe haven for escaped slaves until well into the nineteenth century. By 1800, it had become a more stable maroon community, sheltering former captives from the brutality of South African slavery and existing in part by preying on local farms and traveling wagons. In the words of a visiting Dutch agricultural expert, "a number of these robbers [from Hanglip] watch the narrow and unusually steep pass by night, while others of the band sometimes spend a whole month out robbing, and then in an armed group travel the country with bloody hands and rob this farm and that and plunder it when shown resistance."[7]

Slavery became a dominant institution in South Africa in the early years of permanent Dutch settlement. Intending to maintain cordial relationships with nearby Khoekhoe communities in order to ensure regular supplies of cattle and sheep, the Dutch East India Company opposed their enslavement. Furthermore, with ample land and livestock in the early years of European settlement, few Khoe had reason to work for the newcomers. Thus, following the model already established in its East Indian colony, the VOC turned to the familiar institution of slavery to provide sufficient workers to sustain economic life in the colony. Despite the prevalence of slavery, however, most Europeans owned relatively few slaves—in contrast to the United States and the Caribbean, in which sugar and cotton plantations required a substantial work force.

By the early eighteenth century, slavery thrived in Cape Town and nearby farms and vineyards, where the private demand for labor was substantial. Following the first smallpox epidemic that ravaged the Khoe population, the number of enslaved people grew rapidly and continued to climb as the Cape economy expanded during the latter part of the eighteenth century. Between 1690 and 1795, the number of privately owned slaves soared from 350 to at least 16,839 and to 25,754 three years later in 1798. By then, slaves were more numerous than free burghers, the Company employees who had been released from their contracts and given land to enable them to provide the VOC with vegetables and grain at fixed prices.

Sustaining this labor force required a continual new import of captives, who came from the East Indies, India, Madagascar, and Mozambique. Unlike the settlers, whose reproductive rate was high, enslaved people did not reproduce in sufficient numbers to maintain their population. Though poor diet and living conditions, hard physical labor, epidemics, and disease provide part of the explanation, high infant and adult mortality rates and an imbalance between women and men also explain the need for new supplies of slaves. By the late eighteenth century women still formed only 25 percent of the enslaved population (as opposed to 40 percent of the burgher population) and were less numerous in rural areas than in Cape Town.

The predominance of men among Europeans, especially in the early colonial period, favored the creation of a mixed race population. Because the Company slave lodge served as Cape Town's main brothel, many children with European fathers and slave mothers were born during the seventeenth and eighteenth centuries. Furthermore, in the initial years of settlement Dutch authorities did not discourage intermarriage between free black women and European men, who favored Bengali partners in the seventeenth century and later preferred Cape-born women of mixed ancestry. On the isolated farms of the frontier,

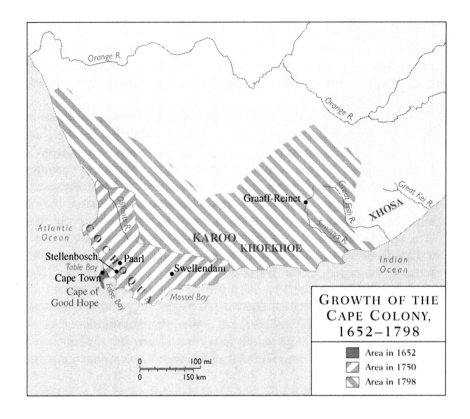

Orange R.

Orange R.

Great Kei R.

Great Fish R.

Graaff-Reinet

XHOSA

Atlantic
Ocean

COCHOQUA

Olifants R.

KAROO

KHOEKHOE

Sundays R.

Indian
Ocean

Stellenbosch ● Paarl
Table Bay ● Swellendam
Cape Town
Cape of
Good Hope

False Bay

● Mossel Bay

GROWTH OF THE
CAPE COLONY,
1652–1798

0 100 mi	▓ Area in 1652
0 150 km	▨ Area in 1750
	▧ Area in 1798

where there was considerable racial mixing, but little intermarriage, relationships between European men and Khoekhoe women produced a
new group of people known as "Bastaards." Their children and those of
slave–Khoekhoe unions were numerous by the late eighteenth century.

The continual shortage of labor in the colony made it extremely difficult for enslaved people to gain their freedom, particularly in the rural
areas. Those freed in the countryside were mainly household slaves,
often women, who might be liberated when their master died. On occasion, European fathers purchased the freedom of their children who
were born to slave women. Several laws kept these numbers low, however, since those who were freed were required to be baptized, speak
Dutch, and have someone who would cover the expenses of poor relief
if necessary. Generally, children born to slave women remained enslaved
all their lives as did the children of women slaves and Khoekhoe fathers.
After 1775, those with slave fathers and Khoekhoe mothers were indentured until the age of twenty-five years. Nonetheless, the population

of "free blacks" gradually increased throughout the eighteenth century to 15 to 20 percent of the free population. With the majority of the enslaved coming from Madagascar and Asia rather than Africa, the term "black" at this time had a different meaning than in later periods of South African history.

Recognizing the crucial place of slavery in the South African economy, J. W. Janssens, the governor in 1804, warned that ending slavery would "destroy all property and plunge the colony into misery."[8] By contrast, the graphic accounts provided by late-eighteenth-century British traveler John Barrow, admittedly a critic of the settlers, suggest that the misery that slaves endured far outweighed what abolition might bring. Recording his travels in southern Africa, he wrote that "The country slaves . . . are ill fed, ill clothed, work extremely hard, and are frequently punished with the greatest severity: sometimes with death, when rage gets the better of prudence and compassion."[9] He continued by saying that "if a black should only strike a white, he runs the chance of being tortured and torn in pieces, on presumptive proof that his intention was to murder; but if a white man murders a black belonging to himself, he puts him into the ground, and nothing more is said about it;—if he murders that of another, he only has to pay the owner his full value. . . ."[10]

Although the South African economy depended heavily on enslaved labor, the nature of the slaves' work differed in the city and the countryside and between enslaved people of varied origins. Most of those enslaved were concentrated in Cape Town, where they worked as domestic servants, artisans, dock workers, gardeners, and nurses; in nearby farming areas they sustained the wheat farms and vineyards. Slaves in private households cooked, cleaned, and hauled water and firewood, with a small minority in the luxurious homes of high officials, wealthy families, or Dutch Reformed ministers. But the British naturalist and explorer William Burchell also described hierarchies among the enslaved population. He observed that the "Malays," who were trained for the more skilled occupations, saw themselves as "superior to all other slaves" and looked down on the nominally free Khoe as "a very inferior race." Those from Mozambique and Madagascar were consigned to "the most laborious" employment.[11]

Cape agriculture, dependent mainly on grain, wine, cattle, and sheep, was more varied than in the Americas, where vast sugar and cotton plantations sustained the slave economy. Supervised by whites, South African slaves sometimes worked up to ten or twelve hours a day, and more during the plowing and harvest seasons. Those residing on farms worked at a variety of tasks: sowing, plowing, and harvesting grain or cutting, pruning, weeding, and picking and pressing grapes in the vineyards. At peak labor times, farmers might hire additional slave or Khoekhoe workers and co-opted women and children for field labor. Enslaved women worked regularly at domestic chores and as seamstresses and wet nurses; they also grew vegetables and milked cows. Children, too, were put to work, helping in seasonal labor and looking after younger children.

Rural living conditions were crude and difficult. Enslaved people usually lived together in large rooms, sleeping on wooden bunks or, on small farms, in kitchens, attics, barns, or even outdoors. Food supplies were often meager, and by the eighteenth century the "tot" system—in which portions of wine were distributed to slaves throughout the day—was becoming established on the wine farms. Though slaves were normally given a shirt and trousers, many were clothed only in rags and they rarely had shoes or hats.

The punishment inflicted on the recaptured followers of Leander Bugis reflected the harsh attitudes toward those who were enslaved. Under the laws of the Dutch East India Company, masters held absolute rights of ownership over their slaves, who, like livestock, were regarded as property and were required to obey orders. Telling his nephew to go ahead and strike one of his slaves with a spade, one sadistic owner said that "I bought him with my own money, if he dies from the blow all I need to do is buy another one."[12] Unable to make legal contracts, slaves were forbidden to marry, had no rights over their children, and could be sold at will. Unlike the situation in the Americas, however, enslaved people were able to give evidence in court, even against their masters, although not under oath; not surprisingly, their testimony was often challenged.

The system's stability rested on the threat or use of force, usually in the form of corporal punishment, most commonly whipping with a *sjambok*, a three-foot strip of hippopotamus or rhinoceros hide. Theft, assault, attempts at escape, neglecting work, and any other forms of "insolence" might provoke such punishment; rubbing salt into the inflicted wound intensified the pain. Other punishments were more brutal, but not uncommon: breaking slaves on the wheel, pulling out pieces of flesh with red-hot tongs, mutilation, impaling, and slow strangulation. In theory, a master who inflicted more than thirty-nine lashes or who failed to provide sufficient food or clothing for a slave might be punished, but in fact external authorities exercised no control over such matters until the nineteenth century. Many farms were too isolated for effective outside intervention, even if authorities had wished to take action. Furthermore, fear of attack from individual slaves or from gangs of runaways so pervaded the rural areas that severe punishments were regarded as necessary to deter rebellion. Masters were convicted of abuse only on the rare occasions when they confessed to having beaten a slave to death. Even in Cape Town intense fears of slave gatherings prompted a 1754 law that imposed a curfew on the enslaved. Legislation also forbade slaves from riding horses or wagons in the streets, singing, whistling, or making noise in the evening, meeting in bars, buying alcohol, or gathering at church entrances during services.

Coming from diverse geographic, linguistic, and cultural backgrounds and, in rural areas, scattered on widely dispersed farms, the enslaved in South Africa found collective revolt difficult to organize. As in all such societies, however, individual and small group attempts at escape occurred frequently, as did other forms of resistance. Criminal records document numerous cases of slaves engaging in theft or sabotage—refusing to work, organizing work slowdowns, burning property, or killing livestock. In a dry climate, setting fire to thatched roofs was an easy way to destroy a master's house. Although surprisingly few slaves physically attacked their masters, a number of mutinies occurred on ships bound for the Cape in the seventeenth and eighteenth centuries. Like these captives, foreign-born slaves, who had known a life of freedom and were less likely to have family or social networks in South Africa, were more likely than the locally born to commit suicide. Despite the low incidence of collective revolt, fear of violence and rebellion was endemic, with rumors sometimes warning that Khoekhoe and slaves were plotting joint attacks. Legal records suggest that the incidence of escape was higher than that of rebellion, though, as the maroon community at Hanglip demonstrates, escaped slaves found survival difficult. To many enslaved people, however, flight may have seemed the only way to escape the back-breaking demands of labor at peak harvest and sowing seasons and during periods of economic expansion.

Because they came from a range of geographic areas and were widely dispersed on small farms in the rural parts of the colony, it was also difficult at first for slaves to develop a common language or a distinctive culture. Although the Dutch custom of naming people based on their area of origin might have preserved some indication of a person's background, this link provided a slender basis for collective identity. In Cape Town, however, with closer contacts among slaves, an environment emerged that was conducive to the development of community, especially in connection with the growth of Islam.

Cape Town itself, clustered at the foot of the dramatic 3,500-foot-high Table Mountain, combined a formal European urban landscape of whitewashed houses, market squares, church steeples, and impressive public buildings with a vibrant underclass culture. Impressed with the town, an early eighteenth-century traveler wrote, "Nothing can be neater, or more pleasant, than the appearance which this town presents." Though not paved, the more than twenty streets intersecting at right angles "are kept always in excellent order, and derive an agreeable freshness from trees of oak and pinaster, planted here and there on either side. The houses are built of brick, and faced with a stucco of lime: they are decorated in front with cornices and many architectural ornaments."[13] In the shadow of these stately buildings, marginalized groups, including free blacks, slaves, political exiles from the East Indies, European soldiers and sailors, and Chinese traders (generally ex-convicts who were considered free blacks) developed a lively urban subculture centered in the city's numerous taverns and based on drinking, gambling, smoking dagga (marijuana), illegal trading, dancing, and music.

Alongside these recreational pursuits, Islam provided a more respectable identity. Brought to the Cape by servants, prisoners, and slaves from Dutch possessions in the East Indies, Islam began to thrive in an eighteenth-century environment in which, apart from a small number of baptisms among Company-owned slaves, little effort was made to convert non-Europeans to Christianity. This reluctance to encourage conversion was particularly strong after 1770, when the Dutch government in Batavia ruled that slaves who became Christians could not be sold. This measure reinforced a widely ignored 1618 ruling by the Dutch Reformed Church "that those who had been baptized ought to enjoy equal right of liberty with the other Christians."[14] The arrival in Cape Town of several Muslim *imams*, religious leaders, who performed marriages and funerals among slaves and free blacks, encouraged the development of the religion. By 1799 the Muslim community petitioned authorities for permission to build a mosque. Carl Peter Thunberg, a late eighteenth-century traveler at the Cape, described a religious ceremony with "priests" in which the congregation read, sang, and recited from a great book, which he presumed to be the Quran: "About eight in the evening the service commenced, when they began to sing loud and soft alternately, sometimes the priests alone, at other times the whole congregation. After this a priest read out of the great book that lay on the cushion before the altar, the congregation at times reading aloud after him."[15]

By the late eighteenth century Dutch conquest had created a culturally heterogeneous, highly stratified society based on slavery and other forms of coerced labor and on resources wrested from indigenous Cape inhabitants. Despite their diverse origins, the social and economic divisions among Europeans were less stark than those between them and subordinate populations. Nonetheless, abundant land, which beckoned some Europeans to seek opportunities outside the confines of Cape Town and its immediate hinterland, created new divisions between those able to emulate European forms of domesticity and the more impoverished frontier settlers who were in many ways becoming Africanized. Everywhere forced labor created a society that relied heavily on individual violence to enforce order. European portrayals of Khoekhoe and San as belonging to a "heathen," subhuman species laid the groundwork for new racial and class distinctions that would emerge fully in the nineteenth century.

CHAPTER 3

New Frontiers

In 1808, Louis, a Cape Town slave who worked as a tailor and was married to a free woman, led a remarkable rebellion against slavery. Following plans hatched with two Irish sailors for the Dutch East India Company, who assured him that there were no slaves in Great Britain or America, Louis traveled into the countryside with his two supporters. They deserted him on the morning the uprising began. But Louis, posing in the uniform of a Spanish sea captain with a smart blue jacket and ostrich feather hat, began marching from farm to farm informing slaves that the governor had ordered their freedom. Christians, he announced, should be bound and brought to Cape Town; they would be shipped overseas and their land distributed to the enslaved. By the end of the day, well over three hundred people had joined the marchers, who moved quickly, but relatively peacefully, gathering arms and ammunition, horses, and wagons; on a few farms they smashed furniture and windows. Most notable in the testimony of those captured that evening was the explanation of their motivation. The Secretary of the Court of Justice reported that all those taken into custody "without exception, declared that they had not the least reasons for complaints against their masters, but on the contrary they had been well treated."[1] Rather they were expressing a profound desire for freedom. Nearly three decades were to pass before these dreams were realized.

Conflict over land, resources, and political power dominated South Africa's history in the nineteenth century just as it did in the United States. In the southwestern Cape and its expanding frontier areas, such clashes during the 1600s and 1700s had confronted the country's sparsely settled indigenous people with difficult choices. Those who survived the smallpox epidemics and the loss of their livestock might resist militarily, assimilate into European society as menial laborers, or withdraw to more distant, less fertile land. During the nineteenth century, however, an increasing number of European settlers began to encroach on the densely settled, often well-armed, farming and herding communities that occupied the rest of southern Africa. This expansion, combined with the concurrent rise of new African kingdoms, generated political and military conflict that, by the 1860s, had drastically changed the political, racial, ethnic, and cultural landscape.

Global competition added a new dimension to the region's history beginning in 1795, when Britain seized Cape Town. The British returned the Cape to the Dutch in 1803 when the threat of a French takeover had receded but recaptured Table Bay in 1806. In addition to the southern tip of Africa, the British had recently acquired India and now dominated the world both economically and militarily. During the first half of the nineteenth century, the most crucial effects of the British seizure of power included legal changes relating to Khoekhoe and slaves, the arrival of influential groups of Christian missionaries, strong economic expansion, the importation of British settlers to the eastern frontier, and the closely connected intensification of conflict with Xhosa communities in the eastern Cape. Responding to these changes, some descendants of earlier Dutch settlers began trekking farther into the interior, thereby expanding the boundaries of European settlement.

The industrial revolution, which had begun in the late eighteenth century, formed the basis of Britain's economic strength. This new system of production, based on free labor, helped to challenge the country's earlier dependence on slavery. Equally important, ideas of liberty promoted in the American and French revolutions coincided with a religious revival whose proponents called themselves humanitarians. Opposed to slavery and the slave trade, humanitarians felt responsible for ensuring that indigenous peoples in the colonies were protected from settlers who relied on enslaved and coerced labor. In 1807 their influence led the British to outlaw the slave trade; the ban took effect on January 1, 1808, the year of Louis's uprising.

Despite the abolition of the slave trade, slave owning continued as a central institution in Cape Town and nearby farming areas, where wine, now encouraged by the British, continued to dominate as the leading commodity. As the demand for exports rose, the exploitation of all farm laborers increased. Under a proclamation issued in 1809 by the Earl of Caledon, then governor of the Cape, Khoekhoe were expected to work more intensely, as were enslaved women, children, and older people. Responding to the heavy demands for labor, officials passed new laws to curb "vagrancy," a term applied to people who wandered around without permanent residences. They now issued passes to Khoekhoe who were seeking work or traveling and gave *landdrosts*, the Dutch term for the local magistrates who administered the law, the right to "apprentice" children and young adults on the farms where they had grown up.

Under humanitarian pressure, however, these harsh measures were moderated. During the 1820s new legislation made it more difficult to split up the families of the small number of enslaved Christians and a newly appointed guardian of slaves began to hear formal complaints about harsh or arbitrary treatment. In 1825, another slave insurrection led by a man named Galant crystallized the social tensions that this brutal institution continued to produce and also revealed the complex relationships between masters and slaves. Unlike the 1808 rebels, who expressed few grievances against their masters, Galant, a twenty-six-year-old slave with a fiery personality, was incensed by repeated floggings that had left his body striped with scars, and by the futility of his complaints to local magistrates. He described one such appeal: "The Landrost called us in and my master said that everything I said was lies. I asked the Landrost to be allowed to speak, but he said he held short proceedings, which consisted in a flogging."[2] Rumors of emancipation had made Galant hopeful about the possibility of change. Although this aborted uprising caused temporary panic in the colony, the rapid capture of the rebels and the hanging of their leaders left another slave rebellion without immediate results.

In addition to regulating the lives of slaves and menial workers, British authorities faced continual problems with independent African communities. Responding in part to intensified clashes with the Nguni-speaking Xhosa on the eastern frontier, the new colonial government imported four thousand British immigrants, settling them in this border area as a way of reinforcing the British military presence there. Based around Grahamstown, these new arrivals, many of them artisans and traders, saw emigration from Britain as an opportunity for economic advancement. With many Methodists among them, these British transplants embodied the values of hard work, discipline, and sacrifice at the heart of their religious value system. Turning at first to trade with their nearest neighbors, many began exchanging food crops such as maize and sorghum for the buttons and beads that the Xhosa used as currency.

Within a decade, the importation of merino sheep had begun to transform the economy of the Cape. Because technological advances in textile production formed a key element of Britain's industrial revolution, the long, silky wool of these Spanish sheep became the "golden fleece" of South Africa's export trade. Also adapting to a new economic environment, the settlers' Xhosa trading partners now desired new goods such as blankets and ironware as well as the arms and ammunition that they would use—ultimately in vain—to protect their land from white incursion.

Alongside these settlers came Protestant missionaries. They established a permanent presence on the eastern frontier in 1803. Imbued with an intense evangelical spirit, they saw free trade and free labor jointly as the avenue to salvation. Abolishing the slave trade in 1807 lent a sense of moral purpose to Britain's imperial ambitions, suggesting that colonization involved a spiritual and ideological commitment to indigenous peoples overseas. In South Africa they directed their main efforts to ending all forms of coercive labor in areas under British control. The pioneers in this effort were London Missionary Society (LMS) representatives such as T. J. van der Kemp and James Read, both of whom married Khoekhoe women and lived apart from the colonial social order in the Cape. They attracted many Khoe converts and, by establishing self-governing local churches, encouraged the emergence of a group of Khoe evangelists who preached and proselytized among their own people.

The most influential LMS missionary of the early nineteenth century, John Philip, arrived in 1819. The son of a Scottish handloom weaver, Philip believed fervently in the superiority of "Christian civilization"; but unlike later Europeans, he connected this superiority to religion and culture, not to race. In his view, indigenous African Christians were capable of becoming "civilized"—which meant adopting not only Christianity, but also European ideas of education, clothing, family life, and the roles of women and men. "Civilization" also required a commitment to the values of hard work, acquisition of material goods, and "respectability," which implied living an upright life devoted to these imported cultural ideals. Coming from an eighteenth-century background that emphasized the ways that people were molded by their surroundings, Philip and his contemporaries saw the "backward races" as having the potential for full rights of citizenship, but as limited by their environment. In his two-volume book, *Researches in South Africa*, he wrote, "We are all born savages, . . . it is the discipline of education, and the circumstances in which we are placed, which create the difference between the rude barbarian and the polished citizen."[3]

Once he arrived in South Africa, Philip worked tirelessly with mission stations all over southern Africa to lift all economic restrictions, including those on labor that slavery promoted. Working together, business leaders and humanitarians promoted many legal and administrative reforms in South Africa; they introduced English common law

*Dr. John Philip and his delegation of Christian Africans went to London in
the 1830s to testify before a Select Committee on Aborigines.* Museum Africa,
Johannesburg.

alongside Dutch Roman law and replaced Dutch administrators with
more liberal British officials. The impersonal jurisdiction of the courts
as the basis of individual rights quickly began to replace the paternalistic authority of the master–slave relationship as the basis of social
order. This pressure led to the passage of Ordinance 50 in 1828, which
applied primarily to the Khoekhoe. Under this law, they received the
right to buy and own land and to agree to entering into service contracts. The law also required parental consent before children could
be taken on as indentured workers. No longer required to carry passes
to move from one place to another, Khoe could now travel to seek
better working conditions. A later regulation against vagrancy that
would have controlled their movement was overturned by the British
government.

Both in Britain and in the colonies, humanitarians detested the
institution of slavery, but they also believed firmly in property rights
and in the need to maintain order and social divisions in society. Thus,
although it was becoming less profitable, they were not inclined to

abolish slavery hastily. A bloody 1831 slave revolt on the West Indian island of Trinidad shocked the British Parliament into action, however, leading the government to rule two years later that slavery should be ended throughout the empire. Under this act, as of December 1, 1834, the 38,000 slaves at the Cape were to become "apprentices" for a four-year transitional period and, at the time of emancipation, their owners were to receive compensation from a fund established in London. Until the 1880s, the descendants of slaves celebrated Emancipation Day as a joyous holiday. But without capital to purchase land, these workers, finally freed completely on December 1, 1838, were released into new forms of poverty.

With slavery ended, both Khoekhoe and those formerly enslaved became exploited workers with few rights, especially in the rural areas. Both groups and their humanitarian supporters argued that without available farm land emancipation meant little. One farmer near Stellenbosch, for example, criticized those who granted "patches of ground to the late apprentices, with permission to erect huts thereon for large families," describing their actions as the "main cause" of the labor shortage.[4] Yet authorities and land owners in the Cape preferred to have these laborers remain an impoverished, seasonal workforce dependent on employers for food, housing, clothing, and access to land—as well as the alcohol they received under the "tot" system. Their movement was controlled by Masters and Servants laws, first adopted in 1841, which granted these workers legal equality; but they suffered the prospect of heavy criminal penalties for breaking their labor contracts or for disobeying or resisting their employers. The ever-present demand for a subordinate workforce became a key element of the new postemancipation regime.

In these difficult circumstances, religious communities offered the formerly enslaved and the nominally free Khoekhoe, both increasingly identified as "coloured," ways to gain control of their own lives and to earn a respected position in society.[5] Many fled their former masters and moved to mission stations, onto vacant land, and into towns—where they hoped to receive higher wages and, whenever possible, to keep married women and children out of the labor force. Keen to adopt European ideas of respectability, they dressed in European-style clothing, took advantage of missionary classes to learn to read the Bible, and sought out mission chapels to formalize their marriages and legitimize their children. High rates of infanticide also suggest that many young women sought to publicly follow standards of Christian morality by appearing not to have babies out of wedlock.

Islam also provided an important alternative avenue for earning respect and status, particularly in Cape Town. Though Islam was well established in South Africa, the first mosque, designed in the style of a Dutch Reformed chapel, was built only in the 1850s. Early nineteenth-century slaves often converted to Islam as a way of rejecting the religion of their masters; but even after emancipation the religion retained an anti-European character, reflecting the local saying, "The Islamic church is the black man's church."[6] Many aspects of Muslim life—dress, diet, religious practices, and the acceptance of polygamy—reflected the distinctiveness of their lifestyle, marking clear boundaries between Islam and Christianity. Yet, while Europeans regarded Muslims as exotic, their abstention from alcohol and emphasis on literacy and education reflected values of self-discipline and social control similar to those of the missionaries.

The same spirit of escape from white domination attracted some four thousand Khoekhoe and freed slaves to a newly created settlement north of Fort Beaufort on the Kat River in 1829. Though the British Commissioner General intended the settlement to be a colonial bulwark against the Xhosa, whom he had expelled from this land, the people who settled there quickly exercised some influence over their own lives by requesting the outcast James Read as their minister. From this influential community, which lasted for several decades, came a new group of indigenous converts who became teachers, artisans, and traders. They brought Christianity and western ideas to new mission stations farther north, opened schools, and, through their political advocacy, helped to create the basis of a new "Hottentot" or coloured identity. Although by the 1850s the project had collapsed, a victim of settler land grabbing, the leader of a failed rebellion to protect the community expressed the spirit that had animated the uprising: "We are now going to stand up for our own affairs. We shall show the settlers that we too are men."[7]

This revolt, known as the Kat River Rebellion, fed into controversy in the Cape Colony over voting rights for a representative Legislative Council. After successfully scuttling a British proposal to make the Cape, like Australia, a port of transport for convicts, the colonists turned to another successful effort—to make the Cape Colony self-governing. In 1853, after heated debate, all adult men, regardless of race, were granted the right to vote provided they earned £50 per year or owned property worth £25. This more open voting system met the interests of both English-speaking liberals and Dutch farmers who hoped that coloured voters would support them against the wealthy British men in the towns. (It is worth recalling that until 1884 Great Britain had a property-based system of voting with higher qualifications and that no Western country permitted women to vote during the nineteenth century.)

The 1820 settlement of British colonists in the eastern Cape put severe new pressures on Xhosa communities living in the fertile pasture and farming lands bordering the Fish River. The First Frontier War, which broke out in 1781, initiated a series of devastating military clashes over land and cattle. By 1856–1857 the joint pressures of British officials, traders, and missionaries combined with drought, famine, and severe cattle illness to generate widespread prophetic beliefs that the ancestors would return to restore the imagined tranquility of precolonial times. Although designed to oust the European invaders from Xhosa soil, they ended by almost destroying the local society.

Military clashes, first with the Dutch and then with the British, initiated this cataclysmic spiral of events. By the late eighteenth century, the Xhosa east of the Fish River lived in small states whose leaders competed for power and resources. Warfare among them, based on the short throwing spear (the assegai), was relatively tame, however. The goal was not to kill your enemies or to expel defeated forces from their land, but to capture cattle and women. These quarrels drew the Xhosa into conflicts and alliances with the colonial powers to the west of the river—first the Dutch and then the British. Having incorporated many Khoekhoe into Xhosa social and political networks in earlier times, Xhosa leaders confidently assumed that they would create similar cooperative relationships with Europeans, including marriage alliances with the daughters of officials. Yet the cultural expectations of the two groups were diametrically opposed: the Xhosa preferred an open frontier, whereas colonial authorities wanted to establish well-defined boundaries. Similarly, the Xhosa looked to customary procedures such as marriage and payments of tribute to their chiefs to cement alliances, whereas Europeans aimed at conquest and the establishment of control over newly seized land. The wars generated by these differences, lasting more than half a century, focused particularly on competition between men for land and cattle. One Xhosa man who grew up in a contested area explained: "When our fathers, and the fathers of the Boors [Boers], first established themselves in the Zuurveld . . . they were brothers—until the herds of [amaXhosa] increased so as to make the hearts of the Boors sore. . . . Our fathers were men: they loved their cattle: their wives and children lived upon the milk: they fought for their property. . . . The white men hated us, but could not drive us away."[8]

These conflicts in the early nineteenth century produced new struggles for leadership within Xhosa communities. In the course of one such competition, Ngqika and his uncle Ndlambe each tried to strengthen his position through strategic alliances with Boer commandos and British authorities. But neither claimant to power was able to halt British land seizures in the eastern Cape between the Kei and Keiskamma rivers. Equally ineffective were the efforts of Makhanda, also known as Nxele, a prophet who combined Xhosa religion and Christianity to create his own religious system. Though attracted to Christian ideas, he also recognized that missionaries would never perceive him as an equal—and would certainly reject his claims to divine power and his view of the world as a battle between the God of the whites and the more powerful (in his eyes) God of the blacks. He also rejected theft, sorcery, and warfare, explaining to a missionary that his spear was "a bloody weapon, and that he must throw it away." [9]

As colonial pressure on the Xhosa continued to mount, during a period of severe drought, Nxele began to preach that one day people who had died would return to earth, bringing an end to witchcraft. His ideas were rooted both in Christianity and in the concept of death and rebirth in the natural world. At the height of Nxele's power in 1819, he led an attack on Grahamstown, ending up imprisoned on Robben Island where Eva had lived her final days. When he and a group of companions drowned in 1820, in a futile effort to escape their incarceration, many Xhosa refused to believe he was dead and were convinced that he would reappear as a black Christ, whom they called Sifuba-sibanzi, the Broad-Chested One.

From the 1820s onward, partly because of the new settlers clustered around Grahamstown, the stresses on Xhosa society increased. In 1829 another scorching drought that drastically limited grazing land added a new dimension to the conflict. During the same year, colonial authorities expelled Maqoma, one of the Xhosa leaders, from his land in order to create the Kat River settlement. Another expulsion in 1833, with theft of cattle as a pretext, left many Xhosa furious, convinced that the colonists' true intent was to seize their land. The arbitrary nature of the "commando" system—by which farmers could take Xhosa cattle at will if they claimed that theirs had been stolen—intensified tension, as did general European scorn for Xhosa leaders. Believing in white cultural superiority, British officials refused to treat chiefs as equals. Whereas in the past their lives had been sacrosanct, they now feared for both their personal safety and the survival of their positions. The officer who brought Maqoma the news of his expulsion reported the ruler's reaction: "He distinctly said . . . that he could not make out the cause of his removal, and asked me if I would tell him; and I really could not; I had heard nothing; no cause was ever assigned to me for the removal."[10] Fueled by these grievances and believing that he was in imminent danger of attack, Hintsa, the leader of all Xhosa communities, whom Europeans called a "paramount chief," launched the war of 1834–1835.

This bitter nine-month struggle, in which British forces murdered Hintsa, was followed by the seventh Frontier War in 1845–1846, led by Hintsa's son Sandile. In the course of these wars, Xhosa spears and shields gradually yielded to greater use of firearms and horses. As Xhosa fighters mastered the art of guerrilla warfare by making strategic retreats to the rugged Amatola mountains, British forces found it difficult to track them. Women, vital in local military conflict, supplied food and ammunition and carried essential messages between commanders and fighters. While the Xhosa remained effective against British troops, their subsistence economy was threatened as colonial forces burned down houses, destroyed crops and stores of grain, and killed cattle. They finally ceased fighting not because of British superiority on the battlefield, but because people were starving and demoralized. Seeking sustenance, growing numbers of Xhosa retreated into the Cape Colony offering to work for Europeans.

During more than fifty years of intermittent warfare, the Xhosa had lost large tracts of their most fertile farming and grazing land, leading to overcrowded settlements. In this uncertain and difficult atmosphere, a new and deeper rift was replacing the division between chiefs and commoners: a gap between the "school" community clustered around the mission stations whose members were drawn to European clothing, schools, and technology, and those who sought to preserve more traditional ways of life. Among the pioneering Christian leaders was Tiyo Soga, who studied in Scotland and became an ordained Presbyterian minister. Though he married a Scottish woman, he always instructed his seven children to take pride in both aspects of their heritage, telling them: "For your own sakes never appear ashamed . . . that you inherit some African blood. It is every whit as good and as pure as that which flows in the veins of my fairer brethren. . . . You will ever cherish the memory of your mother as that of an upright, conscientious, thrifty, Christian Scots woman."[11] In addition to these social divisions, British economic encroachment was causing inflation in bridewealth payments, forcing many couples to postpone marriage.

When the newly appointed governor, Sir Harry Smith, marked out a large Xhosa area as "British Kaffraria" in 1847, he annexed new land, which was then distributed to Europeans and to African refugees

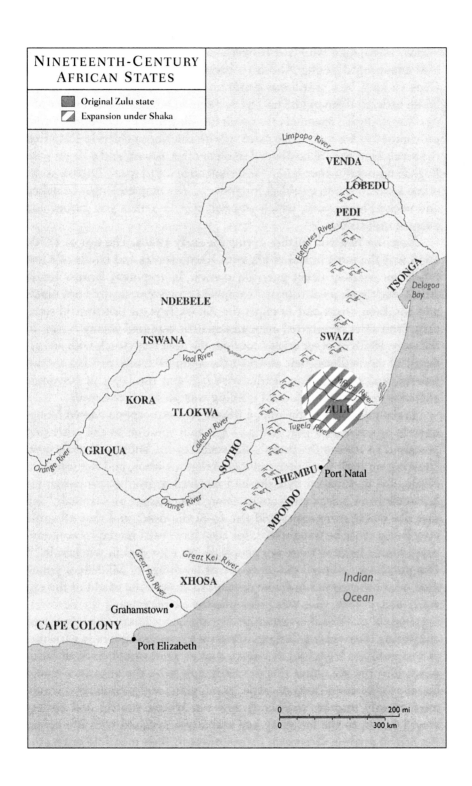

NINETEENTH-CENTURY
AFRICAN STATES

Original Zulu state
Expansion under Shaka

Limpopo River

VENDA

LOBEDU

PEDI

Elefantes River

TSONGA

Delagoa
Bay

NDEBELE

SWAZI

TSWANA

Vaal River

Mfolosi River

ZULU

KORA

TLOKWA

Caledon River

Tugela River

GRIQUA

Orange River

SOTHO

Orange River

THEMBU

Port Natal

MPONDO

Great Kei River

XHOSA

Great Fish River

Indian
Ocean

Grahamstown

CAPE COLONY

Port Elizabeth

0   200 mi

0   300 km

known as Mfengu who had cooperated militarily with the British. He also encouraged young Xhosa to become indentured servants in the Cape Colony. In a gratuitous gesture designed to humiliate the chiefs, Smith ordered them to kiss his feet as a sign of submission to his authority. Describing his agenda in the condescending tone of the period, Smith proclaimed in his first public meeting with the Xhosa chiefs in 1848 that the area's land should be divided into counties, towns, and villages with English names. Furthermore, "You shall all learn to speak English at the schools which I shall establish for you. . . . You may no longer be naked and wicked barbarians, which you will ever be unless you labour and become industrious."[12]

Tensions rose still further during the early 1850s. The war of 1850–1853 was the most brutal of all, with Xhosa forces and bands of Khoe rebels successfully using guerrilla tactics. In response, British forces struck back with a coordinated campaign to systematically burn maize and sorghum crops and to expel the Xhosa beyond British-held territory. Both sides committed atrocities against captured enemy forces. In the early 1850s another crisis occurred; the area was struck with an epidemic of cattle illness that attacked the animals' lungs, causing a slow, painful, and excruciating death. With cattle at the heart of economic and social relationships, social stability was further threatened.

In the midst of this turmoil, a fifteen-year-old orphan named Nongqawuse announced a practical and spiritual solution to the crisis that promised to restore the precolonial social order, but at a terrible cost. Drawing on both Christian and local religious ideas, and the legacy of Nxele, she announced that she had received a prophetic message for her uncle from a dead paramount chief. The message proclaimed: "Tell that the whole community will rise from the dead; and that all cattle now living must be slaughtered, for they have been reared by contaminated hands because there are people about who deal in witchcraft."[13] Her prophecy followed the more recent teachings of Mjaleni, a young man who believed in his divine mission to cleanse the world of the evil substance, *ubuthi*, that was poisoning the earth, causing the devastating drought of 1850. This message also announced that if people ceased cultivating their fields and slaughtered their livestock (already perishing in vast numbers from lung sickness), a great wind would drive all Europeans into the sea. After this dramatic upheaval, the ancestors would be reborn; an abundance of cattle, grain, guns, and ammunition would miraculously appear; witchcraft and evil would vanish; and society would return to the harmony and stability associated with life before the British arrived. Desperate for solutions to their manifold crises, the

A rare photograph of the prophetesses Nongqawuse and Nonkosi, taken in Grahamstown after their capture. During this time they were staying in the home of Major John Gawler, whose wife dressed them up and took them to a photographer. In October 1858 they were confined to the former Paupers' Lodge. Their fate after the prison was dismantled in August 1859 remains uncertain. National Library of South Africa.

community quickly divided into the "believers" in the prophecy (*ama-thamba*, "soft ones") and the "unbelievers" (*amagogotya*, "hard ones"). The first group, the believers, defended an older way of life based on communal solidarity and a willingness to sacrifice the self for the good of the community; the second group, the unbelievers, regarded as selfish and greedy, represented those who had benefited from the opportunities for acquiring wealth in the new colonial order.

The results of Nongqawuse's vision were catastrophic. Fields went unplanted, an estimated 400,000 cattle were killed, and 40,000 people died of starvation. Survivors poured into white areas in search of food and work and the long years of fierce military resistance to colonialism collapsed. The crisis deepened the gulf between those who retained their belief in Xhosa traditions and those who lost confidence in their culture and converted to Christianity—which previously had attracted mainly social misfits and women seeking to escape unwanted marriages.

Although the Xhosa continue to disagree in their assessment of the impact of Nongqawuse's prophetic movement and its aftermath, a local poem eloquently sums up the consequences of this catastrophic event:

> Oh! Nongqawuse! . . .
> She killed our nation
> She told the people, she told them all
> That the dead will arise from their graves
> Bringing joy and bringing wealth
> But she was telling a lie.[14]

By contrast with the Xhosa, their Nguni-speaking northern neighbors, who came to identify themselves as Zulu, created a strong new kingdom in the early nineteenth century that held out longer against colonial conquest. During the late eighteenth and early nineteenth centuries, severe drought and famine helped to foster political consolidation as small states similar to those of the Xhosa began to coalesce around strong leaders. New possibilities for trade, with both the Dutch and British to the south and the Portuguese on the northern coast at Delagoa Bay, also encouraged greater centralization of power. But without shared borders between Zulu lands and the Cape Colony, the European presence did not pose the imminent danger that it did to the Xhosa. Just as Ndlambe and Nxele had vied for power in the Xhosa states, the area to the north generated competition among three rulers, Sobhuza, Zwide, and Dingiswayo. With military rivalries growing more intense in the early nineteenth century, it was no longer possible to continue the customary initiation ceremony, which removed young men from the community to be circumcised and instructed in the responsibilities of adulthood. Instead, these groupings of young men according to age were gradually transformed into military regiments, *amaButho*, whose members were expected to fight together.

Into this tense situation Shaka was born. The diverse and lengthy oral traditions about him differ on the details of his childhood; but all agree in identifying his mother as a woman named Nandi and in emphasizing his difficult youth. Some of these traditions come directly from African oral sources carefully recorded in the later nineteenth or twentieth century; others were filtered through the imperfect memory of both Africans and Europeans. As with all historical sources, written or oral, those who reported these narratives often had a more or less overt political agenda. And, as in many tales of heroic figures, changes that occurred gradually over time were attributed to a single reign. In a similar fashion, a legendary emphasis on overcoming insurmountable difficulties lends these heroes a larger-than-life quality.

Shaka reputedly grew up tormented by other children, forced to move from place to place with his mother in search of refuge. As a young man, he fought with the forces of Dingiswayo, ruler of the Mthethwa. Although not the rightful heir, when his father Senzangakona died in about 1816 Shaka staged a coup and seized power over the small Zulu state. Within a brief period he had reorganized the army and increased its size. After Zwide ordered the assassination of Dingiswayo in 1817, Shaka became the successor to his mentor's kingdom. Traditions recall him as an innovative head of state who made fighting more deadly by introducing the short-handled stabbing spear and a new military formation in the shape of a cow's horn that allowed troops to surround the enemy. He also used the *amaButho* (regiments) as a standing army that was prepared to fight at all times. In fact, the assegai and Zulu military strategies were already part of Nguni fighting techniques, shared also by the Xhosa, while the new system of regiments was probably a gradual innovation, begun under Dingiswayo.

Shaka's rule created a highly centralized and militarized society. Soldiers postponed marriage until after their military service; women, also organized into regiments, remained in their fathers' homesteads but took part in some military campaigns and married as a group when the king granted them permission to do so. During this time, select royal women past childbearing age acquired a new source of power—as the king's appointees in charge of military installations. According to legend, Shaka remained unmarried, apparently fearing heirs who might challenge his position. Some traditions report that any young woman

This widely reproduced engraving of Shaka entitled "Chaka, King of the Zooloe" was based on a drawing by James King, a trader who visited the Zulu kingdom in the mid-1820s. It was published in Nathaniel Isaacs's 1836 book, Travels and Adventures in Eastern Africa. *Museum Africa, Johannesburg.*

who became pregnant by him was put to death. By using cattle captured in war to extend the networks under his control, Shaka was able to assert new authority over the heads of extended families; as clans lost power to the centralized state, a new "Zulu" identity began to replace older local and regional loyalties. Even this highly centralized power was insufficient to protect Shaka from jealous rivals, however; in 1828 his chief advisor and his half-brother Dingane arranged his assassination, and Dingane assumed control of the Zulu kingdom.

Until recently, most European accounts portrayed Shaka as a bloodthirsty tyrant who massacred thousands of captives, engendered terror in his own subjects, and caused neighboring peoples to flee from his armies, causing the depopulation of large expanses of the South African interior. This impression was strongly shaped by the writings of European visitors to his court, such as Nathaniel Isaacs, who was shipwrecked on the Natal coast in 1822. Eager to encourage British intervention in the region, Isaacs wrote of Shaka: "Thus the eve of going to war was always the period of brutal and inhuman murders, in which he seemed to indulge with as much savage delight as the tiger with his prey. When he had determined on a sanguinary display of his power, nothing could restrain his ferocity. . . . He seemed a monster created with more than ordinary power and disposition for doing mischief."[15]

But historians now recognize more varied and complex sources of social disruption. They include white settlers from the northern and northeastern Cape who raided African communities for labor; slave and ivory traders from Portuguese-controlled Delagoa Bay on the northern coast in present-day Mozambique; and Kora (a Khoekhoe group) and mixed-race Griqua attackers. Furthermore, the settlers who appropriated African land in the 1830s and 1840s on the interior plateau known as the highveld may have found the story of Shaka's devastation a convenient way to justify their occupation. These expansive grasslands became the Afrikaner republics of the Orange Free State and the South African Republic (ZAR), also known as the Transvaal, which were founded by discontented Afrikaners who left the Cape in the late 1830s.

Although Shaka profited from the trade in ivory with the Portuguese at Delagoa Bay and was in contact with British traders, he ruled his domain independently with little external interference. Some versions of his death, however, feature prophecies about the future. According to one fictional account, Shaka made the following prediction: "You are killing me in the hope that you will be kings when I am dead, whereas you are wrong, . . . because *umulungu*, the white man, is coming, and it is he who will rule you, and you will be his servants."[16] Indeed, his successors, Dingane and Mpande, faced completely different challenges. As Afrikaner and British colonists advanced into the area, the newcomers took advantage of local power struggles. By enlisting Afrikaner military assistance, Mpande attacked and expelled his half brother in 1840 and was proclaimed king by the Afrikaner leader Andries Pretorius, who had led a slaughter of Zulu troops two years earlier. During his thirty-two-year reign as the Zulu king, Mpande had to accommodate increasing European encroachment on his kingdom.

The upheavals in the Zulu area produced several new kingdoms during the 1820s and 1830s. Sobhuza, one of three competing northern Nguni rulers, fled to the mountainous areas northwest of the Zulu. He transformed an earlier state into what became the Swazi kingdom, where an Nguni-speaking aristocracy adapted Zulu military tactics to rule over the local Sotho population. Sobhuza's successor, Mswati, encouraged intermarriage among different clans in order to create a more unified, centralized state. Mzilikazi, who began as one of Shaka's military commanders, rebelled against the king's authority and fled with several hundred followers across the Drakensberg mountains. Using Zulu fighting techniques and discipline, he built a cohesive community of people from both conquered communities and refugees who joined them voluntarily during the 1820s. They became known as Ndebele. Under attack by white Trekkers in 1838, Mzilikazi fled once again into present-day Zimbabwe. As in the Swazi kingdom, government rested on a system of regiments, which helped to assimilate young men of conquered clans into Ndebele language and culture. Distributing royal cattle and captured young women as wives also promoted loyalty among Mzilikazi's followers. One of the few women leaders of the period, MaNthatisi, a regent for her young son, established the new Sotho-speaking Tlokwa state in the region to the west of the Zulu in the mid-1820s. Though her own people memorialized her as an intelligent, effective head of state, the rarity of female rulers led her enemies to portray her as a grotesque giant with an eye in the middle of her forehead. In 1853, under the less-effective leadership of MaNthatisi's son, Sekonyela, the Tlokwa were absorbed into the neighboring Sotho state.

North and west of present-day Johannesburg, Tswana states were also caught up in the escalating violence, expanding their territory and centralizing power. From the mid-eighteenth century, when maize became the staple crop in high rainfall areas, the population rose and chiefs grew wealthier in cattle and wives, increasing the conflict and competition among them. After the 1820s, the scale and intensity of warfare accelerated once again, with oral traditions recording an invasion by northern Nguni-speaking people related to the Zulu. Most critical for the region's future, however, was the expansion of one lineage, the Ngwato, into a new kingdom. From the 1850s, under the leadership of Sekgoma and then his son Khama, Ngwato became a stable state whose rulers embraced Christianity.

In 1824, four years prior to Shaka's death, a community of British traders on the east coast had established themselves at Port Natal, now Durban. Interested not only in commerce, they became involved in local politics, took African women as wives or concubines, and claimed rights over large tracts of land. By warning of Zulu militarism and devastation, they hoped to attract British intervention from which they might profit. Following a brief interlude of Afrikaner dominance in the region, the British government reluctantly annexed Natal in 1843. Within a decade the new colony attracted some 5,000 British immigrants who expanded European trade routes farther into the African interior, exporting ivory and generating a new demand for African produce and animal products. After experimenting with cotton, indigo, and tea, they settled on sugar as a profitable crop. Despite their shared British rule, Natal became a colony separate from the Cape in 1856 under a constitution that denied almost all African men the right to vote and, as in the Cape, fixed a property qualification for all electors.

In the Sotho-speaking societies to the west of the Zulu, competition over land, cattle, people, and trade also increased during the late eighteenth century under the impact of successive years of severe drought. With ample stocks of guns and ammunition, Khoekhoe and Europeans raided across the frontiers for cattle and slaves. During the early 1820s, attacks by Griqua and Kora, a devastating famine, and refugees fleeing the expanding Zulu state caused further disruption in the region. More frequent raids for crops and cattle led Moshoeshoe, a young chief's son, to send out scouts to locate a safe haven from this chaos. They found a flat-topped mountain, high enough to stave off attacks, and in 1824 Moshoeshoe led a small group of followers seventy miles through biting cold to the safe heights of Thaba Bosiu, "the mountain of the night." By redistributing wealth in cattle to Sotho-, Zulu-, and Xhosa-speaking newcomers fleeing from turmoil throughout the region, Moshoeshoe created a new nation that attracted people seeking peace and stability in troubled times. Eugene Casalis, among the first group of missionaries from the Paris Evangelical Missionary Society, described him glowingly at their first meeting in 1833: "The chief bent upon me a look at once majestic and benevolent. . . . his eyes . . . full of intelligence and softness, made

Moshoeshoe, ca. 1786–1870, led a small group of followers to form a new mountain-top kingdom in the fertile Caledon Valley. Through thoughtful leadership and strategic alliances with both Europeans and Africans, including French Protestant missionaries, he established the foundation of the present nation of Lesotho. In 1868, he was forced to appeal for British annexation in exchange for protection. National Library of South Africa.

a deep impression on me. I felt at once that I had to do with a superior man, trained to think, to command others, and above all himself."[17]

In the face of numerous difficulties, the residents of the area, who became known as BaSotho (although they incorporated only a small group of southern Sotho speakers), sought to ensure their security. By using plows to work the land, they turned rocky, mountainous terrain into productive villages. Acquiring firearms and horses and seeking missionary advice helped to ensure military and political safety and enabled Moshoeshoe to create a single nation from numerous chiefdoms whose inhabitants spoke several different, though related, languages. Moshoeshoe also initiated a pattern of granting a man and his followers land and twenty to thirty head of cattle in exchange for tribute in labor.

From this refuge in the hotly contested Caledon Valley, an exceptionally fertile grain-growing region that now borders Lesotho and South Africa, the Sotho were increasingly able to trade cattle and grain with both Europeans and Africans in order to acquire horses and guns. They also developed an alliance with French Protestant missionaries who advised Moshoeshoe in dealing with the increasingly complex external forces that threatened his kingdom. Although never baptized, the king showed his openness to new ideas by allowing members of his family to be converted to Christianity. In 1843, he signed a treaty with the Cape Colony that required his cooperation in preserving security and peace in exchange for a yearly stipend as well as arms and ammunition. By the 1850s, however, both British settlers and Afrikaners had begun to see this fertile land as a new region for their own expansion. After confronting a series of European invasions, Moshoeshoe was forced to appeal for British annexation of Lesotho in 1868 in exchange for protection. British defense in what became Basutoland helped to shelter additional land from white settlement; but British rule also strengthened the control chiefs had over their people, inaugurated new forms of direct taxation, and deprived the Sotho of land in the Caledon Valley.

Although cattle provided a political asset that Moshoeshoe and other wealthy men could lend to attract followers, agricultural production formed the basis of the new Sotho state. Thus women's hard work growing grain and other crops formed an integral part of Sotho prosperity in the mid-nineteenth century. Their production of surplus grain was important for trade and provided food during the area's recurring droughts. Women added to their grain stores by making pottery and cosmetics, digging salt, and weaving, or by assisting neighbors in their fields. As elsewhere in southern Africa, the economic importance of women produced a strong incentive to control them, keeping women under the dictates of their fathers and their husbands' families.

Two other new states in the interior emerged from Afrikaner responses to the abolition of slavery. In 1837, announcing the intention of Afrikaners to govern themselves, a fifty-four-year-old failed businessman and Huguenot descendant named Piet Retief issued a manifesto that appeared in the *Grahams Town Journal*. Complaining of "severe losses" from the emancipation of slaves, the document declared that his followers intended to leave the eastern Cape in search of freedom from British control. Although committed to "the just principles of liberty," they were also determined "to maintain such regulations as may suppress crime, and preserve proper relations between master and servant."[18] Retief's statement and the Trekkers' mass migration have assumed mythical status in the story of Afrikaner identity. Escaping from British control formed part of the narrative, but the historical circumstances that produced this exodus of Dutch-speaking settlers were complex.

Between 1834 and 1840, in the estimate of one historian, some 15,000 descendants of the early Dutch, French, and German settlers (including women, men, and children) assembled their horses and livestock. Accompanied also by servants, they piled their household goods, furniture, agricultural implements, and weapons into covered wagons and left the Cape Colony heading to the north and east. Now known as the Great Trek, this massive resettlement has been interpreted since the late nineteenth century as a flight from oppressive British domination, the opening gambit in the formation of nationalist identity. There certainly was discontent over the abolition of slavery, a basic institution of Afrikaner society. Angered at receiving about one-fifth the value of what they deemed their property, slave owners were among the leaders of the exodus.

Though these self-styled pioneers had grievances against the British rulers of the Cape, the reasons for their departure were economic as well as political. (Indeed, only a small minority of Trekkers were actually slave owners.) Complaints included insecurity of land ownership in the face of aggressive claims from English-speaking settlers, landlessness, increasing debt, a severe drought in the early 1830s that had already sent people in search of new grazing land, and favorable reports on the quality of the land from Afrikaner travelers to Port Natal. But, like the men and women who spread across the United States and Australia, these Voortrekkers ("front trekkers") were also responding to population growth and increasing demand for agricultural goods resulting from the development of Britain's global trading networks. A tendency to marry at a young age and to produce large families whose sons expected to claim their own land put additional pressure on resources. As the Voortrekkers made their way into the interior, in small family groups traveling together under the leadership of a senior male, they staked out claims to vast farms of six thousand acres and more. Viewing themselves as representatives of a superior Christian civilization, they had no qualms about fighting Africans when necessary. Nonetheless, they were highly dependent on trade and good relations with African rulers, often exchanging sheep and goats for grain and vegetables; and, despite being heavily armed, they lacked the means to govern large numbers of African subjects.

In the course of this mass migration, the Voortrekkers both fought and negotiated with African communities and leaders, some of whom welcomed them as potential allies. Early on, they clashed with the Zulu in a gruesome battle that the Afrikaners later memorialized with heavy Biblical imagery—as a sign of God's intention to grant them a "promised land" in the African interior. As the group headed toward Port Natal, Piet Retief met with the Zulu king, Dingane, purportedly agreeing that the king would grant the Afrikaners a vast area of land in exchange for cattle and guns. When Retief returned with the cattle, but no guns, he and his party were slain. Eleven days later, Zulu warriors surrounded an unsuspecting group of Trekkers, killing five hundred people and seizing 25,000 cattle and thousands of sheep and horses. After the Voortrekkers spent many months without a competent new leader, Andries Pretorius took over as commandant general in Natal and began preparing for a new battle. In mid-December 1838, after learning that Zulu troops were nearby, a group of Trekker commandos lashed their wagons together in a circle, known as a *laager*, and awaited their attack. In the ensuing Battle of Blood River on December 16 some three thousand Zulu warriors were killed, their blood staining the nearby Ncome river. These terrible encounters hastened the downfall of Dingane and his replacement by Mpande, who was more inclined to cooperate with the invaders.

Although the Afrikaners briefly established a republic in Natal after Dingane's defeat, they moved on after 1843 when the British formally annexed the region. Not until the 1850s did most Trekkers settle down on land seized from Africans and begin to create what became two Boer-controlled states—the Orange Free State and the South African

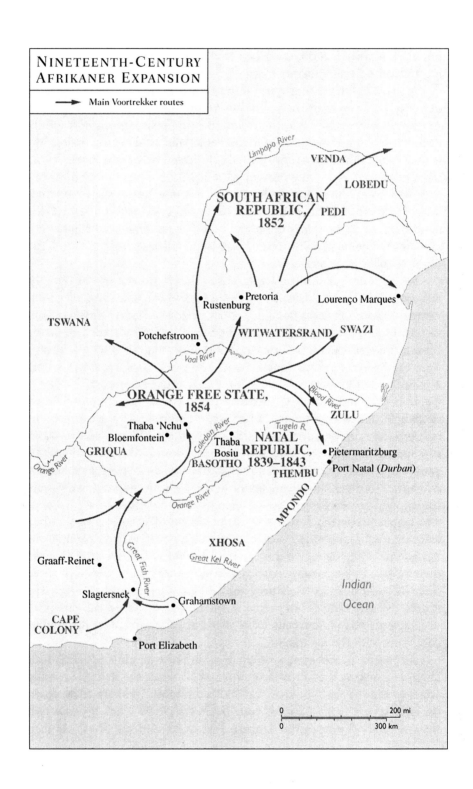

NINETEENTH-CENTURY
AFRIKANER EXPANSION

→ Main Voortrekker routes

Limpopo River

VENDA

LOBEDU

SOUTH AFRICAN
REPUBLIC,
1852   PEDI

TSWANA

Lourenço Marques •

• Pretoria
Rustenburg •

WITWATERSRAND   SWAZI

Potchefstroom •

Vaal River

ORANGE FREE STATE,
1854

Blood River

Thaba 'Nchu •

Bloemfontein •

Coledon River

Thaba
Bosiu

NATAL
REPUBLIC,
1839–1843

Tugela R.

ZULU

GRIQUA

BASOTHO

• Pietermaritzburg

THEMBU

• Port Natal (*Durban*)

Orange River

Orange River

MPONDO

XHOSA

Great Kei River

Graaff-Reinet •

Great Fish River

Slagtersnek •

• Grahamstown

CAPE
COLONY

Indian

Ocean

• Port Elizabeth

0   200 mi
0   300 km

Republic, both of which limited citizenship to white males. The Transvaal constitution, adopted in 1860, articulated principles common to both states, ruling that there should be no equality "of the non-white with the white inhabitants, either in Church or State." Although their constitutions forbade slavery, the new regions thrived on commando raids on African communities for "black ivory"—male children, euphemistically called "apprentices," who were captured and forced to work on white-owned farms.

By the 1850s and 1860s some parts of southern Africa were radically different from what they had been half a century earlier. As British and Boers—colonists and farmers, officials and commandos—appropriated land in the interior of southern Africa, Europeans became entwined in new conflicts and alliances among African states and rulers. Unlike the United States in the nineteenth century, however, no central government annexed the newly conquered lands; instead, two became British colonies (the Cape Colony and Natal) and two (the Orange Free State and the South African Republic) became Voortrekker-ruled republics. Furthermore, until late in the century many African kingdoms and chiefdoms maintained their autonomy from European control.

A complex combination of factors also transformed African societies during this period. These included conflict, consolidation, and alliances that produced major political and religious figures such as Shaka, Moshoeshoe, and Nongqawuse, as well as new forms of trade, conquest, and proselytizing. In the eastern Cape, where missionaries had left the strongest imprint, new divisions developed to replace those between royalty and commoners—a rift between men and women such as Tiyo Soga, who concentrated around the mission stations and began to transform their lives according to Christian–European precepts, and those who continued to follow conventional beliefs and practices. Though the region no longer depended on the labor of imported slaves, their heirs and those of the Khoekhoe (increasingly grouped together as coloured) remained in servile positions with little opportunity for economic or social advancement. Furthermore, particularly in the Transvaal, the children seized as "apprentices" to work on European farms were virtually enslaved. Although the shift from wine to wool as the region's primary export, and continuing European demand for ivory, kept southern Africa linked to the British-dominated world economy, the mineral discoveries of the coming years would effect a far more profound transformation of life in the region—for Africans as well as for Europeans.

Nonetheless, Africans continued to outnumber whites by more than ten to one in the future South Africa, and many African communities remained independent, both inside and outside the British and Afrikaner-controlled areas, and little changed by the conquest of their neighbors. In the early 1860s, for example, the Pedi states of the northeast Transvaal, which would become major players in the mining economy, could mobilize an army of 12,000 men, at least a third of whom were equipped with guns.

CHAPTER 4

Minerals, War, and Unification

The oldest daughter of Sandile, the Xhosa paramount chief, embodied the dramatic changes that transformed South Africa in the last half of the nineteenth century. Born in 1843, she spent her childhood learning the skills of traditional rural life—hoeing and weeding, caring for younger children, and crafting pots, beads, and baskets. In adolescence, along with a group of other girls, she was instructed in the polite, formal behavior expected of married women. Despite this customary upbringing, no record remains of her Xhosa name. Remembered only as Princess Emma, she came to play a pioneering role as an intermediary in addressing the challenges that confronted African communities during her lifetime. Emma was the first Xhosa woman—perhaps the first African woman in South Africa—to own land in her own name. And she paid a high price for her efforts to straddle two diverse, often conflicting societies.

Emma's life began to change when she became one of thirty-five children from prominent Xhosa families sent to a newly established Anglican school in Cape Town. Part of a government plan to transform African societies from above, the school was designed to turn the children of African chiefs into loyal British subjects who would share their mentors' enthusiasm for Christianity and western civilization. The girls, dressed in petticoats, dresses, and aprons, received a less systematic education than the boys at the school, however. Following European customs of the nineteenth century that devalued female learning, the education of girls was intended to provide Christian wives for high-status African men. Despite the shortcomings of her formal schooling, the skills in reading and writing English that Emma learned proved critical to her later in life.

The British concern for appropriate elite marriages did not convince Sandile that he should give up his expectations of receiving substantial bridewealth, *lobola*, through Princess Emma's marriage or of cementing an alliance with another royal family. It also had no effect on the behavior that more traditional communities expected from their rulers. Thus, Emma's life was doomed to disappointment; her first wedding to Qeya, the paramount chief of Thembuland, was called off when his subjects threatened to depose him if he and Emma had a Christian ceremony. Emma already had greeted with dismay Qeya's announced intention to marry more than one wife.

After these plans fell through, Sandile insisted that Emma abandon her skirts and petticoats for a red blanket and ox-hide clothing and arranged her marriage to Stokwe, the son of a minor chief. Although Emma was Stokwe's second wife, her royal heritage assured her of the favored position of Great Wife. After marrying according to Xhosa traditions, she refused to give up many aspects of her mission education, living in a square European-style house, wearing western clothing, and writing letters in English for her husband and other members of the community who were fighting to protect their land from colonial encroachment. Her husband's other wives, nine in all, prevented her from joining a church, however. When both Sandile and Stokwe were killed in the violent rebellions against white authority that flared in the 1870s and early 1880s, Emma (like Eva before her) once again found herself caught between two cultures. She was identified with the Christianized, educated "school people," accused of witchcraft, and forced to flee from her home.

During the 1880s, a time of intense conflict over land, Emma became the only woman to testify before a commission investigating land rights in the Xhosa area. After arguing her own case, she was granted a small farm near Seplan mission for herself and her five children, which became known as Emma Farm. Through similar efforts, she successfully protected her rights to the nearly two thousand acres of land near Middledrift that she had received from the Cape government in 1859—part of a plan to guarantee property to children from elite Xhosa families. Although in her final years Emma joined the church at Seplan, none of her children was raised as a Christian. By the time she died in the early 1890s, the British had crushed all overt rebellion and assumed full control of the eastern Cape.

The final years of Emma's life coincided with complex new developments in the region that would undermine both the achievements and the uneasy compromises of a generation of Africans who were attempting to carve out a respected place for themselves in an increasingly constricted political and social environment. These changes, stemming from the momentous discovery of southern Africa's mineral wealth, coincided with Europe's imperialist "scramble for Africa" and with a severe ecological crisis that helped to break the back of African resistance. The devastating drought of 1876–1879 intensified conflicts over land and resources; in addition, in the 1890s, a combination of disasters (drought, locust attacks, and smallpox) was compounded by a rinderpest (an acute, usually fatal cattle disease) epidemic in 1896–1897 and an outbreak of East Coast Fever from 1904, which together ravaged the region's cattle and made it increasingly impossible for African households to remain aloof from the colonial labor market.

Although the details of conquest differed from place to place, by 1900 all of the region's independent states had come under white domination. Even in border areas, in which Africans might sometimes pit Britons and Afrikaners against each other, the chances for retaining independence were slim in the competitive scramble for territory that dominated late nineteenth-century history throughout Africa, particularly in the wake of the Berlin Conference of 1884, in which the European powers negotiated the boundaries of their imperial claims to the continent. Outright conquest often followed a period in which African rulers drew on white missionaries and colonial officials for military and political assistance in succession disputes or in conflicts with their neighbors, both black and white. Once Europeans were enmeshed in such clashes, annexation invariably followed in one area after the next and African states were forced to cede not only political autonomy, but often large areas of farm and grazing land.

In 1867, two children, Erasmus and Louisa Jacobs, wandering near the banks of the Orange River on a neighbor's farm, discovered a shiny pebble. Experts at first doubted that it was a diamond; but once the stone was positively identified as a twenty-one carat diamond, other discoveries quickly followed in the area that became Griqualand West. Just as gold deposits in California ignited a rush to the west coast in 1848 that remade state and national history, the diamonds unearthed two decades later near present-day Kimberley abruptly transformed South Africa's political, economic, and social life. After gold was found on the Witwatersrand in 1886, at the height of Europe's frenzy for acquiring new African colonies, the region's potential as a sparkling new jewel in the British crown was confirmed, contributing to an escalation of racial and ethnic tensions. From then on, no longer a backwater en route to more lucrative East and South Asian possessions, South Africa became a primary focus of British imperial ambitions. Furthermore, the new wealth intensified the struggles over land and resources that had dominated southern African history since the arrival of the Dutch, exacerbating tensions between Afrikaners and the British and between different African communities striving to protect their interests in the new economic and political environment. In its effects on society, the mining revolution also reshaped and reinforced the racial inequalities so central to South African life.

As in the California gold rush, Kimberley diamonds, the largest deposits in the world, were first excavated by individual prospectors, both black and white, who required little labor, capital, or technology to establish small claims. Initially, African laborers were paid wages higher than elsewhere in the region, which they used mainly to buy guns to help protect their land and political autonomy. But in the mid-1870s, the white Diggers' Protection Association pressured the Cape government, which had laid claim to the area, to exclude black diggers. Thus the mining revolution came to be based on racial exclusion and inequality that would only deepen over time. Furthermore, the system of small, individually owned claims and uncontrolled marketing arrangements did not last for long. Holdings quickly became concentrated and, by the late 1870s, had attracted a flood of foreign investment. By 1891, De Beers Consolidated Mines, controlled by Cecil Rhodes, who had left England for Natal in 1870, had swallowed up all competing interests.

Rhodes, one of nine sons of a parish priest in Hertfordshire, England at first joined his brother on a cotton plantation in Natal. In 1871 they staked a claim in the newly opened diamond fields and in 1888 formed De Beers Consolidated Mines Ltd. Although he returned periodically to Britain to work on a degree at Oxford University, Rhodes devoted the rest of his life to his economic and political concerns in southern Africa. Entering the Parliament of the Cape Colony in 1881, he became prime minister of the Cape in 1890. His forceful and aggressive personality and his grandiose plans to extend British dominion from the Cape to Cairo made him the embodiment of British imperialism. A contemporary journalist and historian described his reaction to this formidable man: "Size was the first external impression you received of Cecil Rhodes. In whatever company you met him he seemed the biggest man present . . . there was something in his leonine head, and the massive, loose pose, which raised him to heroic proportions."[1] Though Rhodes died at the age of forty-eight, his efforts to expand the British empire left a strong imprint not only on South Africa, but also on the colonies to the north that were named Southern and Northern Rhodesia in his honor.

To monitor the labor force and to control theft, the mining companies instituted a system of closed compounds, creating an economy based on migrant labor in which black workers were confined under prison-like conditions and strip-searched at the end of each day. By 1889 overcrowded barracks housed 10,000 African mineworkers. These onerous living conditions, combined with insufficient ventilation underground and poor diet, generated a high death rate from pneumonia. Although white workers were not immune from charges of theft, controlling them was more difficult politically. Collective opposition, particularly from skilled artisans and engine drivers, halted a plan to strip-search white workers, and vocal Kimberley merchants strongly opposed housing white miners in compounds.

While the profits from diamond mining enriched the economy of the Cape Colony and spurred the growth of a complex economic infrastructure, the discovery of massive gold deposits in 1886 in an area of the South African Republic that became known as the Witwatersrand (or the Rand) not only transformed the immediate region but had a wide-ranging impact on the global economy. By the 1890s, the Transvaal was producing between 20 and 25 percent of the world's supply of gold, and mine owners, who in 1889 joined together as the Chamber of Mines, were quickly becoming a powerful political force in both local and imperial politics. Most of the mining engineers who planned the strategies for extracting this wealth, essential to maintaining the value of British currency, came from the United States. With experience both in California and in the new goldfields of Latin America, Australia, and Asia, they advised mine owners not only on how to solve the technical problems of deep-level extraction, but also on the social engineering necessary to recruit and control an efficient labor force.

The new extractive industry reinforced established patterns of migrant labor and racial inequality. As in Kimberley, many African workers were hired on contracts, leaving their wives and children in the rural areas, and confined to cramped (though not closed) compounds. Striking or leaving in mid-contract became a criminal offense, and workers were given signed passes when they left the compound so that deserters could be tracked down. With world gold prices fixed, mine owners struggled continually to cut costs—efforts that would bear fruit in the early twentieth century. Racial divisions were strengthened by the fact that white miners were recruited from all over the world (especially the United States, Australia, and England) and monopolized skilled jobs at wages five times higher than those of Africans. Despite these harsh conditions, by the mid-1890s 100,000 African workers, pushed by new taxes and forced labor recruitment, crowded onto the Rand.

The new city of Johannesburg, which sprang up around the mines, soon eclipsed Cape Town and Durban in size and wealth. As in other mining towns with a largely male workforce, crime, prostitution, and alcoholism flourished. By 1897, in an effort to enforce greater discipline in the workplace, the sale of alcohol to blacks was outlawed. Prohibition did not stop drinking; however, it did attract organized gangs from overseas, including the infamous "Bowery Boys," thugs named after a nineteenth-century New York gang, who encouraged an influx of prostitutes and criminals from the United States and Europe. Only gradually, in the twentieth century, did Johannesburg overcome its reputation as a center of crime and debauchery. The change came in part through official British efforts to attract white women immigrants who, they hoped, would contribute to higher rates of marriage and a more refined and stable family-oriented culture among white men.

Diamonds and gold were not the only sources of demand for workers. Farmers in the east coast colony of Natal were resentful that their Zulu neighbors, able to maintain self-sufficient homesteads under the leadership of indigenous ruling families, had little reason to work on white-owned land. The need for labor on the area's newly developed sugar plantations from 1851 onward, combined with continual labor shortages in the mines, gradually shaped British determination to crush the independent Zulu state. In addition, indentured workers were imported from India between 1860 and 1911 to meet the rising requirements for labor. Under their contracts or indentures, these new immigrants, fleeing the desperate poverty of their native country, added a new ethnic group to the population of Natal. Although brought in for three (later five) years, many remained after their indentures had expired. Their presence also attracted higher-caste Indians to immigrate voluntarily. The indentured workers, including women and children, lived and worked in grim, slave-like conditions, and might be flogged for not working hard enough. Like miners, they required a signed pass to leave the plantation.

At the same time that Natal laws were strictly regulating Indian workers, policies toward the Zulu were also hardening. After the Zulu king, Mpande, died in 1872, the Secretary for Native Affairs in Natal, Theophilus Shepstone, at first sought to maintain British authority by working closely with Cetshwayo, the new king. Shepstone presided over the royal installation ceremony and supported Zulu land claims against the South African Republic. After Britain annexed the Transvaal in 1877, Shepstone sought to gain Afrikaner backing by supporting their claim to the disputed corridor between the Transvaal and Zululand.

Events came to a head when the British high commissioner, in a deliberate effort to provoke war, issued a detailed ultimatum to Cetshwayo that included disbanding his standing army and abolishing the Zulu military system. The ensuing battle at Isandlwana on January 22, 1879 ranks among the most stunning in the history of modern imperialism, as a small British contingent of 822 European soldiers and 431 allied African troops confronted 20,000 Zulu warriors armed with spears and rifles. Using their traditional tactics, the Zulu encircled the British camp and attacked. After a short battle, ending in bloody hand-to-hand fighting, the Zulu triumphed; only a few Europeans survived. Determined not to allow this Zulu victory to stand, the British responded with the full force of concentrated rifle and cannon fire. In the battle of Ulundi on July 4, 1879 Cetshwayo's army was decimated and he was driven into hiding. The *New York Times* reported: "The most circumstantial narrative shows that the Zulus came with a magnificent rush, in dense masses on the rear of the square, and seemed determined to get to close quarters. Their attack on the left flank was not nearly so determined, as that was protected by a Gatling gun, which the Zulu greatly dread."[2] Despite this defeat, the initial Zulu victory inspired the prolonged resistance of both the Sotho and the Pedi, and encouraged the Transvaal under Paul Kruger to reassert its independence in 1881.

After their military triumph, the British divided the Zulu kingdom into thirteen chiefdoms ruled by British appointees and temporarily exiled Cetshwayo to Cape Town. When he died in 1884, a civil war raged, with all sides seeking outside supporters eager to control Zulu land and resources. In 1887, the British assumed full control of what became the colony of British Zululand; a decade later the former Zulu kingdom became part of the Colony of Natal.

British imperialism during the last two decades of the nineteenth century not only destroyed the centralized political system inherited from Shaka, but, by the 1890s, began the process of turning former warriors into wage laborers. As Secretary for Native Affairs in Natal, Shepstone had introduced a "hut" tax that men had to pay in cash for each wife. It became the most important source of revenue in the kingdom. To earn the necessary money, increasing numbers of men were forced to seek work outside their homesteads. Many of these men were recruited by labor agents who worked through chiefs or traveled in small kin-based groups under the supervision of an older relative. Newly absorbed into the ranks of wage workers, they used poetry and song to register their observations about employers and to broadcast this critical information across long distances. They also relied on deeply rooted cultural ideas of *ubuntu*, the hospitality that defined Zulu moral culture and treatment of other people, to develop a militant working-class ethic.

Forming groups called "kitchen associations" (named at first for day workers who gathered together for meals), men gave each other mutual support and protection and adopted guidelines that they expected both employers and fellow workers to follow. On occasion they paraded before the homes of abusive employers shouting out complaints until their demands were accepted. Gatherings to sing and recite poetry promoted a sense of identity and solidarity, turning customary forms of performance into a means of addressing new grievances.

The Zulu rebellion was not yet over in the late 1880s, however. Devastating drought, disease, and cattle epidemics weakened the economies of African households in the following years. In 1905, the Natal legislature instituted a new poll tax on all unmarried adult men. When ordered to pay in early 1906, many Africans refused. Led by a chief named Bambatha (who was killed in battle and decapitated), the Zulu staged their final military resistance. Using scorched-earth tactics, colonial troops devastated the countryside, leaving three to four thousand Africans dead and seven thousand others in prison. These combined assaults on self-sufficient homesteads multiplied the ranks of Zulu migrant labor. From 1907 to 1909, the number of Africans from Natal and Zululand working in the Transvaal increased by 60 percent.

In addition to the battles against the Zulu, conflict raged throughout southern Africa during this period. Concurrent wars in the late 1870s made this a key decade for the loss of African land and power to white encroachment. An epidemic of rinderpest in 1896–1897 further disrupted social and economic life across the region and forced increasing numbers of Africans to become migrant miners and farm laborers.

In the eastern Cape Colony, following the devastating "cattle killing" of 1856–1857, pressure from the Cape government to annex fresh land for white settlement continued, causing new tensions within and among African communities. The final war between the Xhosa and the Cape government, in which more than 3,500 Africans were killed, and rebellions in the Transkei in 1880–1881 failed to halt the annexation process. In the Transkei, however (between the Great Kei River and the Natal border), most land remained under African control, whereas in the Ciskei (west of the Great Kei River) additional land fell to white settlers. In the Kora and Griqua areas near the Orange River conflict was intensified by drought, land claims, and diamond speculation. But even a general uprising in 1878–1879 did not halt the Cape takeover of the region in 1880. Only in 1894, following a civil war over chiefly succession, did the Cape government incorporate Pondoland along the east coast.

Similar conflicts between Africans and Europeans erupted in the northern and eastern Transvaal. In the Pedi area, beginning in the 1850s when the South African Republic (ZAR) tried to impose taxes and labor service on them, many men fled to work in Port Elizabeth in the eastern Cape Colony, planning to return with guns and ammunition to defend their land. They later became the most numerous group of African workers in the diamond fields. While Pedi migrants were seeking the weapons to protect their territory, Sekhukhune, their ruler, became embroiled in disputes with German Lutheran missionaries and their local Christian converts. He resented their criticisms of local religion and polygamy and suspected them of siding with the ZAR whose citizens had seized vast areas of African land. In response to these conflicts, he had the Christian leaders flogged and expelled from the capital. After annexing the Transvaal in 1877, the British demanded taxes and tribute from the Pedi ruler and then attacked with a force that included Transvaal Africans and Swazi soldiers. Once Afrikaner republican government was restored in 1881, skirmishes continued and both Sekhukhune and his rivals for power were killed. These clashes ended the independence of the Pedi state and established the area as a base for workers building the railroad between Delagoa Bay and the Transvaal.

The kingdoms on the eastern highveld also had their independence crushed in the late nineteenth century. The Swazi kingdom to the north of the Zulu fell prey to white farmers and gold prospectors, and finally, in 1902, to British control. In their efforts to counter Zulu attacks, the ruling Nguni aristocracy had formed alliances with the Transvaal, encouraging white farmers to claim land as a buffer with the Zulu; the area was transferred to the British victors following the South African War. By then, only a third of the country remained in African hands. A similar fate awaited communities to the north, such as Lobedu and Venda, which were prime hunting areas for the ivory trade with the coast. Though their rulers tried to hold out against Transvaal power, resistance was crushed by the end of the century.

Like Swaziland, two other states in the region became British Imperial protectorates. In Basutoland (later Lesotho), for which the Cape government had assumed responsibility in 1871 (following the initial British annexation three years earlier), a rebellion broke out in 1880 when chiefs and their subjects refused to relinquish their firearms. In response to a Cape government request, Britain assumed direct imperial control in 1884. For Tswana societies, which included a vast area of the Kalahari desert, the twin pressures of diamond mining and the expansion of Afrikaner farmers led some chiefs to seek external intervention. Britain established the protectorate of Bechuanaland (later Botswana) in 1885, mainly to guard against German annexation.

By this time, however, the Ngwato kingdom had been transformed through its leaders' complex alliance with Christian missionaries. In 1860 Khama, the ruler's son, was baptized and, along with a small group of young aristocratic Christians, adopted the teachings of the missionaries rather than following the traditional path of training as a priest-healer. Khama assumed power in 1875 and ruled the kingdom for fifty years, translating Christianity into local idioms through the leadership of Tswana evangelists. Particularly important were the prayers for rain. In the words of one of these hymns:

> Give us heavy showers
> Pour out raindrops;
> Good rain,
> That is very gentle, not like spears;[3]

In 1895 a deputation of Tswana rulers to Britain, accompanied and assisted by the Rev. William Charles Willoughby from the London Missionary Society, managed to keep the territory under British control, saving it from a takeover by Rhodes's British South Africa Company. But the loss of arable land in the east, combined with the drought and rinderpest of 1896, forced increasing numbers of Tswana to work in the mines.

Although conditions varied from one district to the next, in much of the Orange Free State, the Transvaal, and Natal, where Europeans had seized large tracts of land, many Africans remained on farms as labor tenants or sharecroppers. In subservient and precarious positions, they might continue to plow, plant crops, and graze their livestock on land usurped by white settlers—with the stipulation that they pay a portion of the annual crop to the landlord. While representing a dramatic shift from earlier practices of communal landholding, these widespread arrangements offered tenants some limited space for individual initiative; white settler farmers who attempted to curtail access to land or livestock risked losing their workers to areas still under the control of indigenous chiefs where land was reserved for Africans, or to neighboring farms with less stringent conditions. Although collective resistance among farm workers was almost impossible during this period, there were several alternative means of protest: refusing to pay rent or to perform certain jobs, working slowly, damaging property, or stealing cattle.

Prospects were bleak for most Africans in the late nineteenth century. But small numbers of people (mainly men) were taking advantage of mission schools to create a strong network of believers in the Victorian values of Christianity, a strong work ethic, and individual advancement through Western education. They also took seriously the promise of "Cape liberalism"—the belief that blacks who attained a certain level of "civilization" would be judged on the basis of their accomplishments rather than condemned to inferiority on the basis of race. Among the most prominent of these men was John Tengo Jabavu from the eastern Cape, who worked tirelessly for equality between educated Africans and Europeans. Jabavu was an Mfengu, a group displaced during the disruptions of the early nineteenth century; detached from their roots, many Mfengu were more open to missionary preaching than their neighbors. Through *Imvo Zabantsundu* (usually translated as Black Opinion), the newspaper Jabavu founded in 1884, he supported campaigns against the pass laws, attacked legal inequality and racially biased legislation, and encouraged qualified Africans in the Cape to register as voters. In their unsuccessful struggle to have whites regard them as equals, Jabavu and other educated Christian Africans built European-style brick houses; dressed in European-style jackets, vests, and bowlers; and hung portraits of Queen Victoria on their living room walls. In their leisure time, they became avid cricket and tennis players.

These elite Africans also initiated a new phase of organizing to challenge blatant racial inequalities, both in the political system and in mission churches. Unlike traditionalists, they sought greater opportunity for economic and political advancement within the European-created system rather than fighting against it. In the 1880s, following the final defeat of the Xhosa in the Ninth Frontier War of 1877–1878, Africans in the Cape began to form new organizations to target the eight thousand or so registered voters and to express their grievances and aspirations. Using his newspaper as an organizing tool, Jabavu became a key figure in these political activities. By 1898 a competing group launched a new newspaper, *Izwi Labantu* (Voice of the People), backed by Cecil Rhodes, and a political group, the South African Native Congress. Their leaders, A. K. Soga and Walter Rubusana, favored a strong African political organization rather than a strategy of working with whites to form a single nonracial political party. A similar organization in Natal, *Funamalungelo* (Demand Civic Rights), focused particularly on bringing together the tiny group of Africans exempted through their

In 1884, J. T. Jabavu launched the influential weekly newspaper Imvo Zabantsundu that attacked racist legislation and advocated equality with Europeans for educated Africans. National Library of South Africa.

educational and property qualifications from Native Law, the term for laws administered through traditional authorities.

More widespread expressions of discontent in the 1880s and 1890s came from the African independent church movement known as Ethiopianism, reflecting the belief that the Biblical prophecy "Ethiopia shall soon stretch out her hands unto God"[4] referred to Africans. Disillusioned with the inequities of colonial society, these African Christians, with their insistence on religious autonomy and their rallying cry of "Africa for the Africans," were in many respects more radical than their secular counterparts. The chief adherents of Ethiopianism were the Thembu Church, established in the Transkei in 1882 by Nehemiah Tile, who used the group to express local grievances to the Cape government. Expanding beyond this ethnic base, Ethiopianism quickly spread after Tile's successor made contact with the African Methodist Episcopal (AME) Church in the United States. Following a visit to South Africa in 1898 by AME bishop H. M. Turner, membership rose to 10,000 people. Similarly, a visit to Natal in 1896 by the exuberant American missionary Joseph Booth galvanized support for separation from white mission churches and communicated messages of African equality, autonomy, and uplift that were far more assertive than the polite protests of the contemporary African elite.

The life of Sol Plaatje, born in the Orange Free State in 1876, illustrates most poignantly the strong belief that elite men had in the promise of British culture. His pioneering novel *Mhudi*, set in the 1830s and 1840s, reflected a merging of his literary roots in both local oral tradition and English literature. A journalist, novelist, and political activist, Plaatje became one of the country's most prominent Africans in the first three decades of the twentieth century. One of the founders of the South African Native National Congress (later the African National Congress), he translated Shakespeare into Tswana and Tswana proverbs into English. He also wrote the first novel in English by a black South African. Plaatje spent much of his childhood at the station of the Lutheran Berlin Mission Society located just outside Kimberley, where he worked in the late 1890s as a messenger at the post office.

Then home to a large group of educated Africans, many of them Mfengu from the Cape Colony, Kimberley became a center for the development of their collective consciousness. They were optimistic about the future, believing that imperial British control, which rested with the "Great White Queen" (Victoria), offered hope for legal equality based on "civilization" rather than on race. In an editorial in the *Bechuana Gazette* in 1902, Plaatje wrote: "We do not hanker after social equality with the white man. If anyone tells you that we do so, he is a lunatic, and should be put in chains." But, he added, making a link between race and gender rare for this era: "All we claim is our just dues; we ask for our political recognition as loyal British subjects. . . . Under the Union Jack every person is his neighbour's equal. There are certain regulations for which one should qualify before his legal status is recognised as such: to this qualification race or colour is no bar, and we hope, in the near future, to be able to record that one's sex will no longer debar her from exercising a privilege hitherto enjoyed by the sterner sex only."[5]

Membership in a network of churches, clubs, and societies reaffirmed the strong attraction to European culture of this elite group. Most important for Plaatje was the South Africans Improvement Society, formed to cultivate participants' mastery of the English language and English literature through readings and debates. Expressing his negative assessment of customary African culture during a debate, one member of this organization referred to bridewealth as a "relic of barbarism."[6] Musical events, however, embraced a more synthetic approach, combining African, European, and North American traditions. And, later in life, Plaatje grew deeply interested in the history of the Baralong, the Tswana-speaking group of both his parents. Alongside these cultural activities, sports (particularly tennis, rugby, and cricket) provided exercise and socialization. Both women and men competed at tennis; however, cricket was the preeminent embodiment of the group's aspirations. The game allowed African men to demonstrate their ability to embrace British values by excelling at a sport that demanded deliberation, caution, and patience.

While this complex network of intellectual, cultural, and social organizations helped to forge a common identity that crossed ethnic lines, more parochial loyalties continued to shape attitudes toward marriage and family. When Plaatje defied his parents to marry a Xhosa woman, her family responded indignantly: "What! Is this girl mad that she gives herself away to a coloured boy when there are so many handsome Xhosa boys who loved her? Let them be separated!" His family replied in kind: "Can this handsome boy just go and marry a small Nguni girl when there are so many Tswana girls?"[7]

In the ostensibly "liberal" Cape Colony, the achievements of men such as Plaatje alarmed many whites. The emergence of this group was connected with the dramatic economic transformations in the Transkei, where most land remained in African hands. By the 1870s, a small but growing number of African farmers were becoming relatively prosperous through commercial agriculture. Tilling their fields with plows instead of digging sticks, they began to cultivate substantial crops of wheat, maize, and millet. They also bought sheep and competed with European farmers in selling their wool. On the surface, the emergence of this group of successful Africans demonstrated success in what whites arrogantly termed their "civilizing mission." Yet Europeans feared the consequences of their accomplishments. As the number of prosperous African farmers grew, the number of blacks eligible to vote in Cape elections also increased; indeed, some constituencies approached a black majority. Furthermore, successful commercial farmers had no need to work for others, thereby threatening the supply of cheap black labor for the mines and white-owned farms.

Responding to this perceived threat to white rule, in 1894 the Cape government passed the Glen Grey Act. Proposed by mining magnate Cecil Rhodes, the Prime Minister and Minister for Native Affairs, the act divided the land in the district into individual plots, forcing men without land to work as migrant laborers. On August 15, 1894 an editorial in *Imvo Zabantsundu* supported a petition that urged the Queen of England not to approve the act because this measure "is inconsistent with Your Majesty's treaty obligations with large numbers of Natives who are now forced to surrender their rights to lands occupied by their fathers and themselves, . . . and to pay a labour tax such as is at best a qualified slavery."[8] The act passed nonetheless, but the labor tax included in Glen Grey was dropped a decade later in response to widespread protests, waged in part by Jabavu's newspaper.

The late nineteenth century struggle for territory extended not just to conflicts between white-ruled states and African communities, but also to relations between the British, who controlled the Cape Colony and Natal, and the Afrikaner-governed republics of the Transvaal and the Orange Free State. The gold wealth of the Witwatersrand, located in the Transvaal, contributed to these growing animosities. In 1899, when tensions between the British government and the government of the Transvaal were smoldering, an Afrikaner lawyer, Jacobus de Villiers Roos, published a book (written by the State Attorney of the Transvaal, and later Prime Minister, Jan Smuts), *A Century of Wrong*, in which he catalogued his people's grievances against the British. Denouncing their "lust of robbery" and "spirit of plunder," this republican appeal characterized the Transvaal as a "wounded antelope."[9] Responding to such accusations, the British prime minister advocated war to prove that "we, not the Dutch, are the boss."[10]

These mounting tensions between the British imperial government and the Afrikaner republican states led in 1899 to the outbreak of a violent three-year struggle, sometimes called the second Anglo-Boer War.

By burning houses and fields, the British turned Afrikaner women into both primary victims of the war and adamant opponents of a peace settlement. By creating concentration camps to house displaced women, children, and other refugees from fighting and starvation, the imperial forces also bequeathed a deadly heritage to twentieth-century warfare. After more than two centuries of conquest by both Britons and Afrikaners, these two protagonists turned against each other with all the brutality they had earlier unleashed on African opponents; indeed, British characterizations of their European adversaries as "uncivilized" or "savage" mirrored the racism normally directed toward Africans in the late nineteenth century. Finally, as in many later wars in the colonial world, the Afrikaner republics turned to guerrilla tactics to exploit their more intimate knowledge of the terrain on which they were fighting.

There is no consensus as to whether political and strategic rivalries or economic factors were the primary cause of the war. But clearly southern Africa's newfound mineral wealth was hotly contested. In 1871, Britain had annexed Griqualand West in order to assert control over the diamond fields. Its brief takeover of the Transvaal between 1877 and 1881 ended when the region regained its independence in the first Anglo-Boer War. Thus, the Witwatersrand, the largest source of gold in the world, remained under the sway of the Transvaal and its president, Paul Kruger. Son of a family that had joined the trek from the eastern Cape in 1835, he was a popular politician who believed firmly that "it was God's hand that gave us our independence."[11] In an effort to maintain political power under the control of the original oligarchy, the constitution of the Transvaal disenfranchised men deemed *uitlanders* (aliens or foreigners), including the powerful mining magnates and newly arrived European immigrants. In 1895, when Cecil Rhodes conspired unsuccessfully with his friend Leander Starr Jameson to overthrow the Kruger government, they succeeded only in inflaming anti-British sentiments.

The arrival two years later of a new British high commissioner, the arrogant and unbending Alfred Milner, made negotiations over the franchise more tense and tenuous. By October 1899, convinced that the British were intent on destroying the Transvaal's autonomy, Kruger issued a declaration of war. As the world's strongest imperial power, England was determined to gain control over the region's rich resources and to strengthen its strategic position in relation to the German and Portuguese colonial powers in South West Africa and Mozambique, respectively. Mining interests supported the war, as they had the Jameson Raid, hoping to install a supportive government in the Transvaal.

Race and ethnicity largely determined the response to the impending conflict. Many among the Afrikaner commercial and professional elite, including influential Calvinist ministers, thought of themselves as a "chosen people" singled out to "civilize" a hostile land. The mineral wealth of their new territories reinforced the belief in their divinely appointed destiny. For ordinary farmers, the war involved defending their homes and livelihoods. Most blacks were drawn to the British side, elites hoping for an extension of the Cape franchise to the northern states and farm laborers and miners anticipating improvements in their pay and working conditions. A meeting of coloureds in Cape Town in 1899 reflected the expectation that "no basis for peace will be accepted . . . that does not secure Equal Rights for all civilized British subjects irrespective of colour."[12] Nonetheless, some Africans and coloureds remained in the Transvaal and the Orange Free State as auxiliaries to the troops—bearing and loading guns, cooking, tending horses, repairing equipment, and, on occasion, fighting. Like many blacks, Indians hoped that continued loyalty to the empire would lead to greater justice and equality.

As is common in colonial wars, the imperial power underestimated the abilities and stamina of its adversaries and thought the war would end quickly. But the guerrilla tactics of the Afrikaners and the scorched-earth policies of the British prolonged and intensified the conflict. For the former, this meant splitting up their troops into separate units, attacking trains, clipping telegraph wires, striking British military posts, and turning to smaller battles and nighttime attacks. Early in the war, the British adopted approaches modeled on General William Tecumseh Sherman's march through Georgia during the U.S. Civil War. In an effort to punish families whose men were off fighting, and later to disrupt entire Afrikaner communities and to purge the countryside of all civilians, they burned crops; looted horses, cattle, wagons, and maize; and wantonly smashed their way through farmhouses, in violent actions sometimes at odds with the need to requisition food and supplies for their own troops. When Lord Frederick Roberts, widely known from his stint in Afghanistan as "Butcher Roberts," became Field Marshall of the British forces in South Africa in 1900, he proclaimed that "unless the people generally are made to suffer the misdeeds of those in arms against us, the war will never end."[13] If men continued to fight, he argued, their families would be starved.

By late 1900 the war was creating chaos, with thousands of Afrikaner women and children wandering about the countryside in search of food and shelter. In response, the British authorities created concentration camps to house those who had surrendered as well as for homeless women, children, and old men. Displaced Africans were interned in separate facilities. British aims were not simply meant to house those uprooted by war. Lord Kitchener, the army's chief of staff, perceived Boer farms as "intelligence agencies and supply depots," which fed enemy soldiers and provided them with information about British troop movements; internment, in his view, would pressure men to give up their arms in order to reconnect with their families. Housing some 116,000 Africans and 136,000 Afrikaners, the camps became a battleground for public opinion in Britain, after social and political activist Emily Hobhouse visited South Africa and wrote graphic accounts of the deaths from malnutrition and disease in the white facilities. She described her great shock on a return visit to the camp at Bloemfontein: "The population had redoubled and. . . . Disease was on the increase and the sight of the people made the impression of utter misery. Illness and death had left their marks on the faces of the inhabitants."[14] This devastation challenged the morale of Afrikaner leaders. Plagued by epidemics of measles, dysentery, pneumonia, and whooping cough, more than 27,000 Afrikaner civilians, mainly women and children, died.

Afrikaner women and children refugees during the South African War. By late 1900, a combination of warfare and scorched-earth policies had created chaos, with thousands of people wandering about the countryside in search of food and shelter. In response, the British authorities created concentration camps to house those who were displaced, with separate facilities for Africans and Afrikaners. Library of Congress, LC-USZ62-91953.

War also exacerbated racial and ethnic conflicts. As major victims of domestic destruction and confinement in camps, Afrikaner women became hardened champions of resistance and many men who had been politically indifferent became ardent nationalists. Many blacks had assisted the British from the beginning, as the war went on Afrikaner commandos turned to raiding their homesteads for food and supplies. In response, harassed blacks began attacking Afrikaner troops and fighting on the British side. Indeed, by the war's end, the number of Africans fighting with the British exceeded the number of Afrikaner fighters, and more than 14,000 blacks had died in concentration camps. Furthermore, African tenants on white-owned farms began to occupy abandoned land, threatening to turn the conflict into a peasant rebellion. Indeed, one of the reasons that Afrikaner representatives cited for making peace was that Africans "are mostly armed and are taking part in the war against us, and through the committing of murders and all sorts of cruelties have caused an unbearable condition of affairs in many districts of both Republics."[15]

By April 1902, with many Afrikaner troops ragged and starving, negotiations between the two sides began, resulting in the Treaty of Vereeniging on May 31. Under its terms, the Afrikaner republics agreed to come under the sovereignty of the British Empire, recognizing the authority of the British King Edward VII over a new country that in 1910 would become the Union of South Africa. In the interests, in Kitchener's words, of stabilizing a "reconstructed white settler order," most Afrikaners were granted amnesty, prisoners of war were repatriated, and the British provided nearly £3 million to cover war debts and reconstruction. Milner's ultimate plan was to create "a self-governing white Community, supported by *well-treated* and *justly governed* black labour from Cape Town to Zambesi."[16] To this end, the Afrikaner community would have to be swamped by British immigrants and culturally "denationalized," through Anglicization and modernization. At that point, all of South Africa could become a new autonomous dominion in the British Empire. The treaty expressly excluded Africans from political participation until after the local white community had taken control of the government. In one of many African responses to this decision, the South African Native Congress sent a lengthy petition to the Secretary of State in 1903 expressing its concern that Boers and Britons seemed to have closed ranks against the "alleged black menace."[17]

Thus, although the war produced intense bitterness between Afrikaners and the British, it also forged a commitment to white supremacy that endured for nearly a century, as the British government decided that maintaining its interests in South Africa would depend on collaboration with the Afrikaner majority in the white community. This racially exclusive attitude underpinned the negotiated compromises of the reconstruction period. Both parties to the truce agreed that under the new order black men would be disarmed and disenfranchised, and more stringent pass laws would be reimposed. Returned to their prewar domestic lives, during the coming years Afrikaner women became passionate advocates of ethnically based nationalist politics.

CHAPTER 5

Worlds Apart:
A New Racial Divide

Pixley ka Izaka Seme, born to a Christian family in Natal in 1881, left South Africa in 1898 with plans to study in the United States, following in the footsteps of his cousin John Dube, who had attended Oberlin College in Ohio. With the assistance of the American Congregationalist missionary Reverend S. C. Pixley, whose name he adopted, Seme attended the mission-run Mt. Hermon School for Boys in Northampton, Massachusetts. He then went to Columbia University in New York, where he won the university's highest oratorical honor for a speech entitled "The Regeneration of Africa." After earning a law degree at Oxford University, Seme returned home as an attorney in 1910, unprepared for the shocking treatment of Africans in Johannesburg. Young and self-confident, he reacted with rage when a group of whites objected to his traveling first class on a train and threatened them with a loaded gun. His justification of this impulsive action conveyed his strong class and professional identity. "Like all solicitors," he replied, "I, of course, travel first class."[1] Sparked by this anger, Seme would go on to initiate a new protest organization, the South African Native National Congress, which would struggle for more than eighty years to transform the oppressive conditions in his country.

After the end of the South African War in 1902, the transitional government led by Lord Milner, who served as British high commissioner until 1905, sought to reshape South Africa into an efficient, modernized capitalist state that would promote the interests of mining magnates and ensure continued white supremacy. Sharing the widespread racial prejudices of his contemporaries, Milner proclaimed in a 1903 speech that "A political equality of white and black is impossible."[2]

Milner's cultural and social policies also reflected his determination to anglicize the population and its culture, in part by making English speakers the majority of the white population. His efforts to attract new British settlers to the rural areas and to encourage the immigration of young, single British women, both to replace black men as domestic workers and to provide wives for English-speaking mine workers, were unsuccessful. Perhaps most counterproductive in his campaign for English domination, however, was the attempt to substitute English for Dutch in all government schools—a policy that provoked the formation of new associations to promote the use of Afrikaans, the language that was emerging as a South African variant of Dutch.

In a more dramatic policy maneuver, Milner's administration in 1903 initiated the importation of more than 60,000 Chinese workers to work in the gold mines. With African labor slow to return to the mines after the war because of drastic cuts in wages, the postwar economic boom, and the need to restore their own lands, mine owners began to lobby the government for permission to turn eastward to fill their projected need for nearly 130,000 unskilled laborers. Although in the short run it was more costly to recruit these workers and transport them 12,000 miles than to hire expensive local labor, the mining industry hoped that Chinese miners, employed on longer contracts and without any community support if they deserted, would be cheaper and more pliable workers than their African counterparts.

Once again government policies had unintended consequences. To voice their objections to the threat of new labor competition, prominent Afrikaners created Het Volk (The People) to provide whites with a new political organization. Though working-class white men feared the potential consequences of competition from the underpaid immigrants, their legacy for African miners was immediate. To keep Chinese workers from rising in the labor hierarchy, the mine owners adopted strict guidelines that excluded them from all but the least skilled jobs. When the Chinese were repatriated in 1907, these restrictions were extended to Africans, thereby strengthening the "color bar" in employment that reserved all the better-paid, more highly skilled jobs for whites and once again relegating Africans to the most grueling and dangerous positions deep underground.

In addition to determining who would perform the poorly paid labor that kept gold supplies flowing, politicians confronted the thorny problem of how to unify the two former Afrikaner republics (which briefly became British colonies after the war) with Natal and the Cape Colony. Among the most controversial issues was whether the restricted black voting rights at the Cape (where all men with certain income, property, and literacy qualifications could vote) should be extended to the entire country. Under pressure from the Transvaal, the Orange Free State, and Natal, the delegates to a National Convention meeting to discuss unification reached a compromise by which each province would retain its own franchise provisions. Thus, outside the Cape even the best-educated, most prosperous black men were denied the right to vote. In a similar concession to Afrikaner fears and prejudice, rural districts were weighted more heavily than the cities in votes for Parliament. And at a time when women were rarely enfranchised, few objected to excluding all women from the rights of citizenship.

While these discussions were taking place, educated Africans such as Pixley Seme were actively organizing, using the powerful slogan "Vukani Bantu" (Rise Up You People) to galvanize their opposition to policies detrimental to their interests. Despite African hopes of postwar reforms in their favor, they soon realized that if Britons and Afrikaners agreed on one issue, it was the continued denial of rights to Africans. This consensus spurred renewed activity among regional groups of the South African Native Congress. In 1909, as the provisions of the South Africa Bill outlining the conditions of union became clear, a restrained and respectful group of activists met as the South African Native Convention to oppose these measures. Hoping to enlist British support, Cape liberal W. P. Schreiner, a constitutional lawyer and former prime minister of the Cape Colony, led a black and coloured delegation to London in 1909. Its members included both John Tengo Jabavu and coloured physician and political organizer Abdullah Abdurahman.

Before the Bill was heard and approved in the House of Commons, the delegates submitted a petition to parliament expressing deep disappointment at the threat to the rights of "coloured people and natives" in the Cape Colony and their fears that racial discrimination throughout the country would be "accentuated and increased." Such provisions, they argued, unjustly disenfranchised people who had shown their "unswerving loyalty to the Crown, their attachment to British institutions, their submission to the laws of the land, and their capacity for exercising full civil and political rights." The only just solution lay in granting political equality "to qualified men irrespective of race, colour, or creed."[3]

Following these efforts to promote greater equality in the newly formed country, Seme and three other English-trained lawyers met to plan for a new protest organization, which became the South African Native National Congress (SANNC). At a meeting in Bloemfontein on January 8, 1912, the SANNC (later called the African National Congress) was born. Located in the center of the country with a well-established black population of educated professionals and skilled workers, Bloemfontein was an appropriate site for a national meeting. Speaking

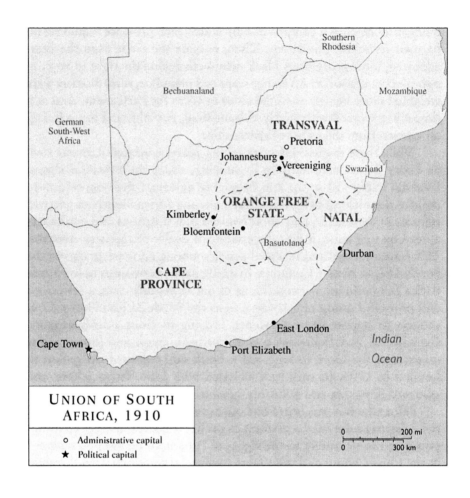

Southern
Rhodesia

Bechuanaland

Mozambique

German
South-West
Africa

TRANSVAAL

○ Pretoria

Johannesburg ●
● Vereeniging

Swaziland

**ORANGE FREE
STATE**

Kimberley ●

NATAL

Bloemfontein ●

Basutoland

● Durban

**CAPE
PROVINCE**

● East London

Cape Town ★

● Port Elizabeth

*Indian
Ocean*

UNION OF SOUTH
AFRICA, 1910

○ Administrative capital
★ Political capital

0   200 mi

0   300 km

passionately, Seme explained the goals of the founding members: "We have discovered that in the land of their birth, Africans are treated as hewers of wood and drawers of water. The white people of this country have formed what is known as the Union of South Africa—a union in which we have no voice in the making of laws and no part in their administration. We have called you . . . so that we can together devise ways and means of forming our national unity and defending our rights and privileges."[4] The policies that Seme and his colleagues invoked reflected the region's long history of colonial conquest and exploitation. But these men and a single woman delegate, primarily ministers, lawyers, teachers, clerks, and chiefs, particularly targeted the South African state, created in 1910, that kept power in the hands of whites. The group

This delegation from the South African Natives National Congress (SANNC) journeyed to England in 1919 to protest the Natives Land Act of 1913. The act strictly limited the areas in which Africans could own land and restricted their right to remain as tenants and sharecroppers on white-owned land. Members of the delegation included, in the back row, Richard Victor Selope Thema, Josiah Tshangana Gumede, and Levi Thomas Mvabaza; front row, Sol T. Plaatje and the Rev. Henry Reed Ngcayiya. William Cullen Library, University of the Witwatersrand.

they launched would have a vital place in shaping African resistance in the years to come.

A year after the SANNC was created its founders would have a new and equally serious grievance, the 1913 Natives Land Act. Although Africans comprised more than 67 percent of the country's population at the time, under this law they were denied the right to own land in all but 7.5 percent of its territory, mainly in overcrowded regions designated as "native reserves." The expansion of this segregated area to 13 percent in 1936 did little to alleviate the resulting congestion and poverty Adopted in part to force Africans to work in the mines, the law also restricted their rights to remain as tenants and sharecroppers on white-owned farms, turning them instead into wage laborers who would be obliged to move if they lost their jobs.

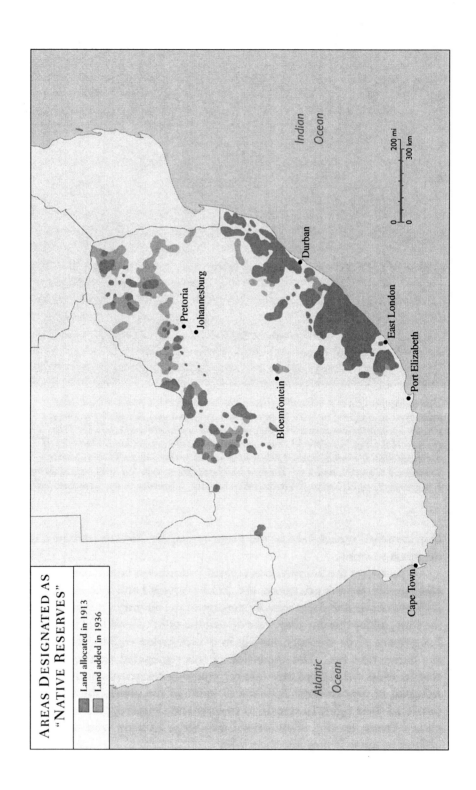

AREAS DESIGNATED AS
"NATIVE RESERVES"

Land allocated in 1913
Land added in 1936

Indian
Ocean

Durban

Pretoria
Johannesburg

Bloemfontein

East London

Port Elizabeth

Cape Town

Atlantic
Ocean

200 mi

300 km

Sol Plaatje, who by then knew many of the white political leaders of the former Cape Colony and who had played a role in founding the SANNC, traveled across the country by bicycle to document the law's effects on the African population, which he outlined powerfully in his classic work *Native Life in South Africa*. As a member of delegations to the British government in 1914 and 1919, he campaigned actively (but unsuccessfully) against the injustice of Africans being denied the right to vote or to buy land in their own country. His book, written to appeal to the British public, opens with these words: "Awaking on Friday morning, June 20, 1913, the South African Native found himself, not actually a slave, but a pariah in the land of his birth."[5] In 1921 Plaatje took his campaign to the United States, where he gave separate talks to the Bethel AME (African Methodist Episcopal) Church in Harlem on "The Black Man's Burden in South Africa" and "The Black Woman's Burden in South Africa"—no doubt a play on the title of Rudyard Kipling's poem that designated imperialism as "The White Man's Burden." His efforts formed part of the ongoing challenge to laws and policies that disenfranchised and oppressed the majority of the country's population.

African protests against racial inequality paralleled similar, but more confrontational, actions among the Indian population. In 1894, following the passage of laws that denied Indians the right to vote, taxed those who remained after their indentures had expired, and created new obstacles for Indian-owned businesses, a young lawyer named Mohandas Gandhi helped to form an advocacy group, the Natal Indian Congress. Twelve years later, when the Transvaal government enacted a measure that required all Indians over the age of eight to carry a pass, thousands of people protested, organizing mass meetings, refusing to register for the documents, and risking arrest and deportation. These militant, but peaceful, actions gave rise to the concept of nonviolent resistance to unjust authority, which Gandhi termed *satyagraha*, meaning "struggle for truth" or "truth force." In 1913, after a new campaign against the tax on formerly indentured women, men, and children sparked violent clashes and led to Gandhi's arrest, the outcry in India (then a British colony) led the South African government to suspend the hated law. In the midst of this publicity, Gandhi returned to India early in 1915 as a hero. Although he never again lived in South Africa, the legacy of nonviolent resistance would inspire not only the successful anticolonial struggle in India, but a later generation of civil rights protesters in South Africa and the United States.

Denied political rights and excluded from the newly formed SANNC, some women also turned strategies of civil disobedience to their advantage.

In May 1913 residents of the conservative, Afrikaner-dominated town of Bloemfontein and small towns across the Orange Free State were startled by the sight of six hundred African and coloured women marching through the streets to protest the laws that forced them to carry passes. Bloemfontein's black location was distinctive with its "wide, straight roads with little square houses more or less European looking. . . . Inside they are many of them extremely neat and comfortable, with lace curtains to the windows, good furniture, and as many pretty knick-knacks and photographs as adorn any English cottage."[6] Although passes were required throughout the country for all black men over the age of sixteen years, only the Orange Free State mandated them for women. The eighty women arrested in the confrontation were protesting a policy that exposed them to abuse and even rape by the police who performed routine pass checks. Capturing their militant spirit, the local African Political Organization (APO) newspaper described sticks striking the skulls of police who sought to stop the demonstrators. "We have done with pleading, we now demand," the women declared.[7]

Passes ignited their anger not only because of potential abuse and harassment, but also because of their effects on family life. By requiring a white employer's monthly signature, the system forced women from their homes and into poorly paid jobs as domestic labor. Most women preferred instead to augment their meager family income by working at home, doing laundry, or brewing and selling beer. One of the protesters, Charlotte Manye Maxeke (the lone woman at the first SANNC meeting), founded the Bantu Women's League as the women's section of the SANNC in 1918, when a proposed bill threatened to extend the pass laws to women across the country. Arrests and trials resulting from the demonstrations and further political pressure on both local and national government officials persisted until 1926, when a court ruling exempted women from having to carry passes because they were not considered "persons" in the eyes of the law.

The continued disenfranchisement of blacks in the Transvaal and the Orange Free State after the war also prompted coloured South Africans to organize their own advocacy group. Founded in Cape Town in 1902, the APO grew quickly under the leadership of Abdullah Abdurahman, the Scottish-trained medical doctor who was part of the delegation to London in 1909. During his long tenure as president, from 1905 to 1940, he was in the difficult position of advocating for a group caught between the temptations of acceptance by whites as more "civilized" than their darker-skinned compatriots and the fact of their political and economic inequality. Complicating their identity, the coloured community was closely related culturally to the Afrikaners: they spoke Afrikaans as their first language and the non-Muslims among them worshiped in segregated Dutch Reformed Church congregations. In addition, their jobs and pay scales placed them above Africans, but below whites, in the country's increasingly rigid racial hierarchy.

In 1914, two years after the SANNC was organized, a group of prominent Afrikaners mounted a counteroffensive to growing British economic and cultural power, launching another new political group, the National Party of South Africa. Appealing to the idea of "nation" as did its African counterpart, these men had a very different agenda for the country—promoting an alliance between the country's two white "races." The party's formation, however, reflected a conflict within the Afrikaner community between Louis Botha, a former general during the South African War whom Britain had appointed as the country's first prime minister, and J. B. M. Hertzog, another former general who launched the new party. Whereas Botha, leader of the South African Party, believed it was politically expedient to promote reconciliation between his people and the British, Hertzog remained bitterly opposed to his wartime adversaries.

When Botha's government followed Britain's lead at the start of World War I and declared war on Germany in September 1914, a small group of disgruntled Afrikaner nationalists plotted a coup. Objecting to Britain's request that South Africa invade neighboring German-ruled South West Africa, the rebels planned to ride on horseback to Pretoria, declare an Afrikaner republic, and win back the country from domination by British-controlled mining interests. Most of the 11,000 men who took up arms alongside the rebels were desperately poor white farmers, many from the Orange Free State, whose farms and livestock had never recovered from either the devastation of the South African War or the drought and disease that followed. The rebellion began inauspiciously, however, when one of its leaders, war hero Koos de la Ray, was killed in a roadblock set up to trap an infamous gang of thieves. With his death, the initial plan was dropped. But in October, after Botha refused a citizen's demand that South Africa withdraw its troops from South West Africa, General Christiaan de Wet summoned commandos in the Orange Free State to resume the revolt. With Botha personally assuming control of government troops, the uprising was crushed within a month, though not the anti-British hostility that had fueled it. Nor did the support of poor white farmers completely mask the hatred that one of them had expressed in 1905 when he condemned rich landowners as "selfish, self-righteous blood-suckers!"[8]

The energy poured into creating a self-conscious Afrikaner cultural identity in the early twentieth century represented a complex response to both nationalism and class. Class divisions within the Afrikaner community, particularly between wealthy farmers and landless *bywoners* (tenants), were acute both in the Cape and in the northern provinces. During the South African War many of the most impoverished men either had refused to fight or had fought on the British side. These divisions hardened in the postwar period, along with a weakening of the kinship ties that had formerly linked the two groups. In response to rural poverty, some entire families were forced to migrate to small towns and cities; others sent their daughters, who were more likely to find work than their elders. Once in urban centers, and outside the strict family bonds of rural life, young people grew more assertive. Many of them questioned their fathers' authority, abandoned the Dutch Reformed Church in favor of smaller, more spirited evangelical sects with greater emotional appeal, and, in impoverished urban neighborhoods, mixed more freely with blacks. Anna Scheepers, who in 1938 became president of the Transvaal Garment Workers' Union (GWU), was typical of these women. She grew up in a family of nine children on a farm near Krugersdorp. After finishing school she spent two years struggling against her father who, despite his losses during the depression, refused to allow her to work in Johannesburg—in his eyes "the place of sin." She finally said to him, "Listen here, don't be foolish. I can look after myself. . . . God will provide for me."[9] After seven months of working sixteen-hour shifts in a delicatessen, a friend got her a job in a garment factory.

Such social transformation created intense anxiety, both within the church and among middle-class moralists who feared that the family was crumbling under the impact of industrialization. Sympathetic to the poverty that threatened poor whites, the five-volume report of the Carnegie Commission on the poor white problem in South Africa argued that for young girls, "the potential mothers of our nation, there is no normal social or home education."[10] As middle-class women's organizations emerged to confront these threats to Afrikaner solidarity, their welfare initiatives helped to promote a strong nationalist identification among poor families. Along with small farmers worried about the growing divide between landlords and tenants and educated professionals angered by Milner's schemes to anglicize South African culture, these changes contributed to a new cultural and political movement that would galvanize Afrikaners of all classes by raising the status of their language and making it the basis of a resurgent nationalist movement.

By the late nineteenth century the Dutch spoken by South Africa's original white settlers had splintered into numerous social and regional dialects, permeated with German, French, English, Portuguese Creole, and Xhosa vocabulary and syntax. As the first language not only of the Afrikaners, but also of the widely diverse coloured community, Afrikaans was scorned by many people as a language of poor whites and servants. During the early twentieth century, however, a group of journalists led by Gustav Preller began to publish in Afrikaans rather than Dutch. Though done in part to increase the circulation of their publications among the less-educated members of their community, by standardizing a middle-class form of Afrikaans and making it respectable, their efforts contributed to ridding the language of its strong associations with impoverished whites and coloureds. These initiatives also prompted an outpouring of books, magazines, newspapers, and dictionaries that lent the language new literary respectability. Under considerable pressure from this "Second Language Movement," in 1918 two universities began to teach Afrikaans as a subject and, in 1925, the government designated Afrikaans rather than Dutch as the country's second official language alongside English.

The process of establishing Afrikaans as a uniform, popularly accepted language went hand in hand with a new emphasis on Afrikaner history, culture, and folklore, in part as a reaction to the growing domination of English popular culture. As poets such as Jan Celliers, Eugene Marais, and Totius poured out fictionalized accounts of Afrikaner suffering during the South African War, writers such as Gustav Preller heralded Piet Retief and other Voortrekkers as heroes, and began to elevate the "Great Trek" as the defining moment of nineteenth-century Afrikaner nationalism. Identifying the family as the primary source of ethnic identity, the enormously popular magazine *Die Huisgenoot* (The Family Companion), modeled after the *Saturday Evening Post*, targeted its messages of Afrikaner marginalization in a British-dominated culture to women. One article decried South African shops, houses, books, newspapers, and schools as "bastions and agents of a foreign culture which claims for itself the right to overrun and conquer the world."[11] To combat this cultural imperialism, *Die Huisgenoot* set out to guarantee that Afrikaner women, in their role as mothers, were creating an appropriately nationalist environment in their homes. Thus the magazine was responsible for creating an "Afrikaner" perspective on sex education, marital problems, and "scientific" approaches to housework and other domestic issues. It also warned women that an Afrikaner child must "speak his own language, know the history of his *volk* [people], be familiar with his Bible. . . . By the seventh year the child must know what the word Afrikaner is."[12]

In 1938, these efforts at creating a unified Afrikaner ethnic identity climaxed in a nationwide centennial celebration of the Great Trek. Beginning in Cape Town, nine or ten ox-wagons retraced the steps of the Voortrekkers' original journey across South Africa with their occupants reverting to the flowing beards, bonnets, and long dresses of nineteenth-century pioneers. Greeted by cheering crowds along the route who staged ceremonies to commemorate Afrikaner heroes, this reenactment of the historic exodus completed the elevation of the Trek to the center of Afrikaner historical consciousness and reinforced the ideology of white supremacy at the heart of South African history. At their journey's end in Pretoria on December 16, 1938 (the anniversary of the Battle of Blood River at which the Trekkers defeated the Zulu), participants laid the cornerstone for the massive granite and marble Voortrekker Monument that captured their odyssey in stone. By becoming a virtual pilgrimage site for a rising Afrikaner "nation," the monument reinforced the nineteenth-century myth that their territorial expansion was divinely inspired. Nationalist leader D. F. Malan explained: "The Great Trek gave our People its soul. It was the cradle of our nationhood. It will always show us the beacon on our path and serve as our lighthouse in our night."[13] With a Ph.D. in theology from the University of Utrecht in the Netherlands, Malan had resigned from the ministry in 1915 to become more politically involved. His main concern was the need to keep South Africa a "white man's country" by elevating the position of poor whites and preventing blacks from competing with them for jobs.

Reflecting such fears about black competition, Afrikaner nationalism contributed to the infrastructure of segregated laws and institutions that were developed during the period between the two world wars. Some of these policies were adopted during the 1920s in the wake of the bloody and divisive revolt of white mineworkers in 1922; others emerged during the 1930s in response to the worldwide economic depression and its aftermath. They included several key features: hardening residential segregation and social separation between racial groups, reinforcing the position of local chiefs in rural African communities, limiting Africans' rights as workers and as voters, and in the wake of the depression, creating new jobs for poor white men, predominantly Afrikaners. Other legislation reinforced these measures by barring Africans from holding skilled jobs; outlawing interracial sexual contacts outside of marriage; and mandating segregation in schools, churches, prisons, health services, and urban neighborhoods. Stricter enforcement

Participants in the centennial celebration of the Great Trek riding in a Voortrekker wagon. The two women and the child are wearing the bonnets of their nineteenth-century forebears. Campbell Collections of the University of KwaZulu-Natal.

of the pass laws put black men under constant police surveillance, making it more difficult for them to move in search of work.

In designing these racially exclusive policies, some South Africans looked to another former British colony with extensive experience in building segregated institutions—the United States. They were particularly interested in models for schooling such as the Tuskegee Institute, where moderate African American leader Booker T. Washington had created a widely respected center of black higher education based on practical training in crafts and agriculture. Washington believed that improved economic skills combined with morality, self-discipline, and self-reliance were more important to gaining political equality than campaigning for greater rights. In a similar vein, C. T. Loram, an influential South African proponent of industrial education, wrote a doctoral dissertation at Teachers College, Columbia University, on "The Education of the South African Natives." He argued that "a weekly timetable which gives two hours for geography but only half an hour to hygiene, which has no periods for gardening or agriculture, and makes no provision other than needlework for the special needs of the girls, is not adequately helping the pupils to adapt themselves to their environment."[14]

Segregation affected rural areas differently than the cities, although labor migration linked town and countryside in complex webs of social and economic entanglement. In the "reserves," the areas designated for African occupancy under the Natives Land Act of 1913, African communities retained their land (which was protected from further white usurpation), but also became heavily dependent on men's wages from migrant labor and women remaining behind to grow food and care for children and older people. Appointed chiefs and headmen, some of whom claimed descent from older ruling lineages, became the backbone of a local administrative system designed to create and legitimize the regime of conservative government-salaried officials who could help to control young people and staunch claims for greater equality. One member of Parliament explained the government's rationale: "An adaptionist policy demands as its primary concept the maintenance of chieftaindom [sic] without which tribal society cannot exist. . . . The adaptionist policy assumes a difference between the Abantu and the Europeans. It assumes some measure of territorial segregation."[15] Afrikaner ethnologists such as W. W. M. Eiselen believed that strengthening the reserves would encourage Africans to identify with their rural cultural backgrounds rather than aspiring to become more Europeanized.

Although created by the white government, chieftaincy also provided the institutional structure and symbols around which groups could allocate land, conduct local court cases, and compete for power. In Natal, with an indigenous royal family, proponents of segregation perceived the Zulu king as a bulwark against radical political change. Despite these intentions, the king, Solomon ka Dinuzulu, often declined to pay deference to Britain. In 1930 he infuriated officials when he addressed the governor general of South Africa by insisting on his own royal blood. "The people at my back recognize me as a Chief of the Royal House of Zulus. Each country has its own King. . . . Some people think they can rule a country by their cleverness but we know that only people of Royal Blood are fitted to rule. Things in this country will never be right until I am recognized as the head of the country."[16]

Labor unrest, both white and black, also played an important part in shaping politics in the period between the two world wars. Two distinct strands came together to make up the lively white working-class opposition to a colonial economic order dominated by overseas interests. One came from British workers, heirs to the militant trade unionism and socialism of the Labour Party in their home country. Often confrontational in their tactics, they aimed to reform the existing system through campaigns for higher wages, better working conditions, and union organization. The men who split from the Labour Party in 1915 to form the International Socialist League favored a more radical opposition to capitalism. These Russian and East European immigrants, often veterans of revolutionary socialist and working-class movements in Russia, Poland, Latvia, or Lithuania, were revolutionaries who argued that class conflict would propel history forward to a socialist future. From this committed core of activists came the Communist Party of South Africa (CPSA), founded in 1921, a small, tightly disciplined group that hoped to overthrow the capitalist state and establish a socialist government in South Africa.

Although the CPSA believed in theory that working-class unity should transcend racial divisions, the group's earliest members were exclusively white, prompting their controversial slogan: "Workers of the world unite and fight for a white South Africa." Changing course after 1924, the Party experimented with several strategies to try to attract black members, first working through the Industrial and Commercial Workers' Union (ICU) founded by Clements Kadalie in 1919 and, from the late 1920s, advocating the formation of an "independent native republic" within South Africa in which blacks could control their own political destiny. From this period also dated the idea of a two-stage revolution by which socialists would cooperate with African nationalist groups to work for racial equality, postponing the goal of socialism until after democracy had been achieved.

Kadalie, a charismatic immigrant from the British colony of Nyasaland (now Malawi), attracted attention with his fiery speeches urging Cape Town dock workers to go on strike. In the surge of recession and unemployment that followed World War I, urban workers quickly embraced his message—that militant action was essential to improving their wages and working conditions. Although he aimed his efforts at black workers, an active working-class and socialist movement made white workers equally receptive to such appeals. But with white wages ten times higher than those of Africans, interracial working-class unity was almost impossible. Always seeking new ways to cut costs, employers' periodic threats to hire more black workers constantly undermined the position of their white counterparts.

Whereas Clements Kadalie began his campaign to organize African workers in Cape Town, Durban, and Johannesburg, the ICU ignited massive popular support only when it spread into the countryside. During the 1920s, rural African tenants, sharecroppers, and squatters faced heavy demands to work longer hours and pay higher rents. At the same time, the land on which they could grow their own crops or graze their herds was being severely cut back as mechanization reduced the demand for unskilled labor.

Realizing that they were losing ground in the struggle to survive on white-owned farms, both men and women flocked into the ICU. Drawn by the extravagant promises of Kadalie and other flamboyant leaders, membership reached a peak of 100,000 in 1927, and red ICU cards became an important status symbol in rural areas. Under the auspices of this group, which combined the economic appeal of a trade union with the emotional exuberance of a religious revival, farm workers campaigned for higher pay, refused to plant and plough, pressured farmers to sign contracts, and supported tenants evicted from their farms and homes. The uncompromising rhetoric of the ICU appealed to men and women who lacked power in their own lives. One newspaper article rallied support by urging disobedience to the established order: "When those in authority become so unreasonably notorious at your expense, disregard that authority, be blind and 'damn the consequences.'"[17] Sharecropper Kas Maine recalled many years later that "The white farmers said that we thought ourselves superior ever since we had started following Kadalie."[18] He himself never joined, however, believing that industrial tactics were unsuited to the countryside. "How can you have a strike in another man's home?" he asked.[19]

Although communist belief in workers' power and class conflict had a strong appeal to these rural laborers, even more powerful was the militant nationalist rhetoric of Jamaican-born black nationalist Marcus Garvey, founder of the United Negro Improvement Association (UNIA), whose ideology was adopted by many ICU leaders. From his base in New York City, where he moved in 1916, Garvey broadcast a message of black pride merged with cultural and economic independence, which made the UNIA an enormously popular mass movement. As chapters spread to South Africa, in part through African American missionaries, its rallying cry of "Africa for the Africans" resonated with downtrodden blacks. Kadalie identified closely with Garvey, to the point of adopting an American accent when he spoke English. In the 1920s, desperate for an end to poverty and exploitation and perceiving black American missionaries as modern and westernized, some ICU members looked to African Americans to drive whites into the sea. Knowing little about the United States, they idealized "America" as a symbol of freedom, a "mighty race of black people overseas, dreaded by all European nations . . . [They] manufacture for their own purposes engines, locomotives, ships, motor cars, aeroplanes, and mighty weapons of war"[20]—symbols of the colonial, industrial world from which they were excluded. Reflecting such racially based nationalism, Kadalie exhorted delegates at the African National Congress (ANC) Annual Conference in 1926: "They [Europeans] spoke of a Native problem. This is no Native problem, but a European problem of weakness, greed and robbery."[21]

Although the ICU developed a mass following in the 1920s, it never mobilized the resources or the organizational strength it would have needed to stave off a decade of government harassment and farm evictions. But the group also crumbled from within, suffering from an inadequate structure, loss of faith when the grandiose promises of leaders failed to bear fruit, and a widespread tendency for leaders to use the organization to enrich themselves. By the time the great depression hit South Africa, a few local groups remained, but the national ICU had faded as an effective political force with a widespread following.

Rural blacks provided one critical source of labor unrest during the interwar years; the other source came from miners. As the cost of living spiraled during the period after World War I, both black and white miners organized massive work stoppages. With the value of gold falling in a time of rapid inflation, mine owners struggled against their employees to sustain their high profit levels. In February 1920, the arrest of African miners for trying to organize a strike triggered a strong chain reaction. Within a short time, half the black miners on the Witwatersrand had joined them in protest against low wages, poor housing, and the color bar, which kept them in the worst paid, least skilled positions. Confronted by troops and police who surrounded the mining compounds, the strikers were forced back to work by the end of the month. White miners in the years to come would not be so easily crushed.

Between January and March 1922, economic activity in Johannesburg almost came to a standstill. In a period of acute financial difficulty, the high cost of white labor led the Chamber of Mines to propose lifting the color bar and moving black workers into formerly white jobs at significantly lower rates of pay. When negotiations broke down, thousands of white mine workers came out on strike and, armed by a small communist group, set up barricades. As a general uprising seemed a distinct possibility, the city of Johannesburg ground to a halt for several months. Related industries ceased production and thousands of miners along with their families and supporters staged regular marches across the Witwatersrand. Only a military assault with troops, tanks, and aircraft brought the miners back to their jobs, leaving hundreds of people dead and wounded, thousands arrested, and four executed. The massive strike affected not only coal and gold miners, but also their families. By late February, relief committees were feeding some 30,000 people. Despite the hardships, in most of the major demonstrations leading up to the army attacks on strikers, women's commandos joined in the processions and sometimes in the violence.

From 1922 on, fearful of another uprising, politicians paid close and nervous attention to their white working-class constituencies. Responding to the widespread panic about another revolt among white workers, the Industrial Conciliation Act of 1924 established new procedures through which white and coloured workers might resolve industrial disputes with their employers. Trade union membership, including the right to bargain over wages and working conditions or to go on strike, was restricted to these two groups and denied to virtually all African men, who were excluded from the definition of "employee." The Apprenticeship Act of 1922 had already made it almost impossible for Africans to become apprentices in most trades. Through other measures, known as the "civilized labour policies," the government also gave manufacturers economic incentives to maintain a set ratio between white and black workers that greatly favored whites. Because women received lower pay than men, these policies sparked rising employment rates among white women in textile mills and garment factories. Under the auspices of left-wing white organizers such as Solly Sachs, young Afrikaner women, including Johanna Cornelius, Bettie du Toit, and Anna Scheepers, became highly committed trade unionists during the 1930s.

From 1933 onward, as the South African economy recovered from the worldwide depression, the government went even further to ensure the loyalty of working-class Afrikaners. By creating new jobs for unskilled Afrikaner men in government-controlled enterprises—railways, the civil service, and the state-run iron and steel corporation—the state effectively wiped out the dire white poverty of earlier years, but left untouched the misery of the majority of blacks.

As a program of affirmative action for poor Afrikaners, these measures formed a critical part of the political response to the Rand Revolt and the depression. By threatening capitalist stability in South Africa, these crises also promoted new alliances between rival political groups. After the Rand Revolt, the Labour Party, which represented working-class whites, formed a coalition with the National Party led by the Afrikaner nationalist General J. B. M. Hertzog, in an effort to staunch discontent among disadvantaged whites. As prime minister, Hertzog was able to hold together this racial alliance, known as the Pact government, between 1924 and 1933. Following the depression and the Labour Party's splintering, a new partnership dubbed the Fusion government assumed power between 1933 and 1939. This merger joined the National Party with the South African Party of Jan Smuts to form the United Party. During these critical years for stabilizing the economy, Hertzog remained prime minister, with Smuts as deputy prime minister. Though also an Afrikaner and one of the intellectual architects of segregationist policies, Smuts differed from Hertzog in that he accepted the framework of British imperial control in South Africa, which many Afrikaners condemned. In 1934 opponents of Fusion, led by the extreme nationalist D. F. Malan, broke with the National Party to form their own, more militant, Purified National Party. Five years later, the Fusion alliance split over the contentious issue of whether South Africa should take part in World War II as Britain's ally, with Hertzog favoring a policy of neutrality between Britain and Germany.

Belief in the dominance of an ostensibly pure white race inspired Malan's break with the Fusion government and his rhetoric. The new party's prime movers came from the Afrikaner Broederbond (brotherhood). Formed as a secret organization in 1918, this group of teachers, academics, clergy, civil servants, lawyers, farmers, and businessmen represented the elite of their community. Broederbond membership was highly restrictive, limited to Afrikaans-speaking white men of "clean character and firm principles"[22] who belonged to one of the Dutch Reformed churches. Their goal of mobilizing a majority of Afrikaners in support of ethnic nationalism and racial purity was not achieved until the 1940s; but electoral success in 1948 represented more than a decade of sustained, well-planned campaigns to control all aspects of national life. These efforts drew on ideas associated with nineteenth-century and early twentieth-century theories of eugenics, which blamed racial mixing for the decline of civilization and biological degeneration. By the late 1930s, as Afrikaner nationalists began to admire Nazi Germany as a model of "racial" purity, such ideas became more elaborate and entrenched, preparing the ground for the postwar policies of apartheid. Before his death in 1942, Hertzog observed that the "true character" of National Socialism in Germany was closely attuned to the "spiritual and religious outlook of the Afrikaner nation."[23]

In this climate of increasingly formalized racial segregation between the two world wars, many Africans turned to religious communities in which they could express their ideas and aspirations apart from white control. At Bulhoek in the eastern Cape, the followers of an independent church called the Israelites established the holy village of Ntabelanga, the Mountain of the Rising Sun. Their prophet, Enoch Mgijima, had summoned them there to await the end of the world, which they expected at any moment. Partially in response to complaints from both white and black farmers, officials accused them of squatting illegally on the land. In a letter to the local magistrate, two members explained their position: "We are not making war against you; we are your servants living in this place for the purpose for [sic] praying and fearing God's wrath which is coming upon the whole world . . . We humbly beg you to give us a chance to pray."[24] In May 1921, when persuasion and intimidation failed to move the Israelites from their village, the government dispatched eight hundred soldiers and police armed with rifles and machine guns to evict them. With only assegais and knobkerries (short wooden clubs with a knob on one end) to defend themselves, nearly two hundred Israelites died.

Groups such as the Israelites represented part of a broad spectrum of African responses to Christian ideas and institutions. Although many Africans joined established mission churches, others were attracted to the creative energy and millennial goals of self-proclaimed prophets such as Mgijima. African women created their own religious culture, joining prayer associations, *manyano*, that helped them to cope with the profound changes occurring in family life, particularly the loss of control over their daughters as customary forms of courtship and sexuality eroded in the face of migrant labor and urbanization. African American missionaries from the African Methodist Episcopal (AME) Church also established a strong foothold in South Africa from the late nineteenth century, first on the Rand and then spreading quickly throughout the country. Through the AME Church, African religious communities forged connections to a wider black identity, particularly in the United States, and to international struggles against segregation and colonization. The black clergy of the AME Church provided a model for African aspirations to leadership and the close connections between African Methodists and the early ANC helped to link religious and political movements. Many of the AME arguments for racial justice were purely religious, however, based on the equality of all people in the eyes of God. On these grounds, one church elder encouraged his congregation to address whites by their names rather than as "Baas," the customary deferential term.

Whether overly political or not, authorities often felt threatened by African-initiated churches. Reacting to the devastating death toll during the influenza epidemic of 1918, which she saw as a form of God's punishment for people's sins, Nontetha Nkwenkwe founded a church in the Ciskei region of the eastern Cape that produced a sharp reaction from the government. In her eyes, individual and collective healing were closely intertwined. Considering herself an instrument of God, she drew on both Christian and local religious ideas to attract followers. When authorities, still reeling from the violence at Bulhoek, confined her to a mental hospital for fear of civil unrest, a group of her followers organized a pilgrimage on foot to Pretoria six hundred miles away in an effort to secure her release. Their efforts failed, however, and Nontetha remained hospitalized until her death in 1935. But incarceration did not dampen her followers' fervent belief in her powers. When the apartheid government released political prisoners in 1990, many of them hoped in vain that she would be among them. In 1998, hundreds of people clad in the distinctive black and white uniforms of her disciples gathered to rebury her remains, which historians Robert Edgar and Hilary Sapire had rescued from a pauper's grave near Pretoria. Because of Edgar's American origins, his arrival was perceived as fulfilling Nontetha's prophetic words to her followers in the 1920s. Reflecting the influence of Wellington Buthelezi, a local disciple of Marcus Garvey who preached that black Americans would arrive to free South Africans from oppression, Nontetha had instructed, "Look to the Americans—they will help you one day."[25]

While both established and independent Ethiopian religious movements drew adherents from across the class spectrum of African communities, new opportunities for western education were creating a sizable African middle class, often in the cities, but also clustered around prestigious educational institutions such as Fort Hare in the eastern Cape. As the first institution of higher education for Africans in the country, Fort Hare, founded in 1916 by Scottish missionaries, became the alma mater of many of the country's leading political figures, most notably Nelson Mandela, who entered the college in 1939 intending to become a clerk or an interpreter in the Native Affairs Department. Fort Hare professors included some of the country's major black political figures such as D. D. T. Jabavu, who taught Xhosa, Latin, history, and anthropology, and Z. K. Matthews, whom Mandela praised as "the very model of the African intellectual."[26]

But before Fort Hare was established, many of these elite men (and a few women) had had to leave South Africa for Great Britain or the United States (often sponsored by church groups) to complete their education. Two of the most prominent among them were A. B. Xuma, a physician trained in the United States who became president of the ANC in 1940, and his close friend Charlotte Manye Maxeke, who founded the Bantu Women's League as the female affiliate of the SANNC. Their time abroad forged another connection with the transnational black cultural movements of the 1920s and 1930s that were creating a "New Negro" identity. These educated women and men also were actively engaged in using their skills to address the social, economic, and political challenges that faced African communities in the era of segregation.

Working-class Africans struggled to shape their own culture in the cities and mines, as Modikwe Dikobe vividly recounts in *The Marabi Dance*, his novel of township life in Johannesburg in the 1930s. Portraying the grim and squalid housing conditions in the cramped slumyards, he wrote that the yard "served a row of five rooms, each about

Clara Bridgman, an American Board missionary, and Charlotte Manye Maxeke, founder of the Bantu Women's League, laying the cornerstone for the Bridgman Memorial Hospital, which opened in Johannesburg in 1928. The hospital provided maternity care for black women and began a program to train African midwives. Campbell Collections of the University of KwaZulu-Natal.

fourteen by twelve feet in size. When it rained, the yard was as muddy as a cattle kraal [enclosure], and the smell of beer, thrown out by the police on their raids, combining with the stench of the lavatories, was nauseating."[27]

Against this bleak setting his characters lived out the tensions and conflicts, but also the cultural creativity and innovation, inherent in urban life during the 1930s. The plot of this novel centers on the characters' struggles to reconcile longstanding rural values about marriage, courtship, religion, and family with the demands of life in a large, heterogeneous city, where men struggled to find and keep jobs working for Europeans, women risked arrest for illegal beer-brewing, and unscrupulous preachers ran off with people's money. Through the story of a young woman named Martha, the narrative juxtaposes the polite, elite society of the schools and the Bantu Men's Social Centre with the more vibrant, undisciplined music and dance of *marabi* culture, which Martha's "respectable" rural-born parents condemned for its association with "persons of a low type." Marabi, a form of music and dance popular in the 1920s and 1930s, blended early African American Dixieland with local South African harmonies and rhythms.

The Bantu Men's Social Centre, based in Johannesburg as it was in the novel, exerted a particularly strong influence through its "Non-European Library" funded by the Carnegie Corporation of New York. In an era when most libraries in the country excluded blacks, its books and recordings exposed a new generation of black writers to the vibrant voices of the Harlem Renaissance, the flowering of African American literature, arts, and culture during the 1920s and early1930s. No one felt this influence more powerfully than the future novelist Peter Abrahams. Describing his reaction to philosopher Alain Locke's historic collection of African American fiction, poetry, drama, and essays, *The New Negro*, Abrahams wrote of his profound inspiration. "These poems and stories were written by Negroes! Something burst deep inside me. The world could never again belong to white people only! Never again!"[28]

As the depression ended by the mid-1930s and the government began to implement new and stricter forms of segregation and disenfranchisement, African political organizations seemed incapable of stopping the enactment of new laws that further entrenched white supremacy. The Hertzog Bills, passed in 1936, abolished the African vote in the Cape, already diluted when white women won the franchise in 1930, and established a powerless new body, the Natives' Representative Council, to voice African opinion. Although African political leaders formed the All-African Convention in 1935 to fight the bills, they were unable to prevent the white members of Parliament from disenfranchising them or to persuade the government to increase further the amount of land added to the African reserves. The delegates' eloquent resolution, which warned that the logical outcome of their actions "will be the creation of two nations in South Africa, whose interests and aspirations must inevitably clash . . . and thus cause unnecessary bitterness and political strife,"[29] fell on deaf ears.

Meanwhile, the ANC had experienced brief spurts of militancy, supporting striking municipal workers and miners after World War I and in 1927 electing the radical Josiah Gumede as president. Reflecting both communist and black nationalist ideas, Gumede advocated "the right of self determination through the complete overthrow of capitalism and imperialist domination . . . the principle of Africa for the Africans."[30] But Pixley Seme, who replaced him as president in 1930, was concerned particularly with improving relations between the chiefs and educated Africans. Only in 1940, when A. B. Xuma was elected ANC president, was there a campaign to revitalize the group from the grassroots. Despite his efforts, the surge of energy that transformed the ANC would come not from the men of Xuma's background, but from a new generation determined to confront the still unresolved issues that had sparked Seme's rage thirty years earlier.

CHAPTER 6

Nationalisms in Conflict: The Rise of Apartheid

In January 1940, Nontsikelelo Albertina Thethiwe, a twenty-one-year-old mission-educated woman, arrived in Johannesburg from the Transkei to study nursing at the Non-European Hospital. Her father had died suddenly in 1929, when she was eleven years old, and she came to the city after rejecting a marriage arranged by her uncle. Although her preference was teaching, Thethiwe loved nursing and caring for patients. In a later interview, she explained, "I wanted to be a teacher. But conditions wouldn't allow me to be a teacher. So I had to take up nursing, where when you are training you are being paid. So my hope was that at least if I am being paid, I will be able to help my brothers and sister."[1] Having grown up in a rural area in which Africans had less daily contact with whites than in the cities, Thethiwe found the racism and segregation at the hospital profoundly disturbing; when the matron refused her request for a leave of absence to return home after her mother's death, she was deeply shaken. The matron behaved, she recalled angrily, "as if a dog had died."[2]

A year later, Thethiwe met Walter Sisulu, the man who would become her husband and who would draw her into the heady political environment of early 1940s Johannesburg. Six years her senior and also from the Transkei, Sisulu was more familiar with politics and city life. His experiences had included a backbreaking stint underground loading ore at a mine, working twelve-hour days for a dairy farmer who, after a quarrel, whipped him with a *sjambok*, a heavy whip, until he bled, and losing his job at the Premier Milling Company when he initiated a strike for higher wages. Such mistreatment opened Sisulu's eyes to the powerlessness of black South Africans and prompted his interest in politics. Attending rallies and meetings, he heard the impassioned rhetoric of Industrial and Commercial Workers' Union leader Clements Kadalie and the more moderate appeals of the African National Congress (ANC) and the All-African Convention. By the early 1940s, when Sisulu launched a new career running his own real estate agency, he was becoming increasingly involved with a group of like-minded young men in the ANC, including Nelson Mandela. Organized as the Youth League, they would challenge their elders and push the organization to embrace a new wave of militancy and mass political organizing. When Walter Sisulu and Albertina Thethiwe married in 1944, another young activist, A. P. Mda, warned the young bride that her husband "was already married to the nation."[3]

Albertina and Walter Sisulu met and married during a wartime period that was critical to deepening the rift between Britons and Afrikaners and between whites and blacks. Following the German invasion of Poland on September 1, 1939, a parliament divided between supporters of Britain and Germany voted to declare war on the Nazi state, putting an end to the brief alliance between Jan Smuts and J. B. M. Hertzog. From then until 1948, Smuts held the office of prime minister under a United Party government. Between 1939 and 1945, World War II created an economic boom that wiped out any lingering remnants of the depression. Local industries began manufacturing uniforms and military equipment, while 300,000 men, predominantly whites, left South Africa to join the Allied forces in North Africa and Europe. With a growing demand for labor, filled only in part by white women, black men and their families flocked into the major cities. In Johannesburg, where the African population rose by 100 percent in the decade up to 1946, housing was scarce, leaving new migrants to squat on vacant land or to crowd several families into cramped two- and three-room municipal houses. Squalid living conditions, low wages, and steep price increases created a volatile political situation.

In response to these pressures, illegal strikes proliferated, political organizations demanded the repeal of the pass laws, and Johannesburg commuters from Alexandra township boycotted buses for seven weeks to protest hikes in fares. In the most militant acts of the 1940s, thousands of men and women seized vacant land and built makeshift shacks of burlap, cardboard, and corrugated iron in an effort to create homes for themselves and their families. James Mpanza, who led the most successful squatters' movement, saw himself as a Christ-like figure, calling his group the Sofasonke ("we shall all die together") party. Although these confrontational protests attracted only intermittent support from the ANC and the Communist Party of South Africa, they generated a widespread spirit of anger and resistance that would help to fuel new demands for political equality as the war wound down.

As magnets for rural migrants, the cities attracted not only those seeking factory work or fleeing from drought, starvation, and land hunger, but also educated Africans for whom "Egoli" (the City of Gold, as Johannesburg was known) offered educational and professional opportunities unavailable in the countryside. Women and young men also were attempting to escape the paternalistic controls wielded by their elders. Like Albertina Thethiwe, Nelson Mandela ran away to Johannesburg in the early 1940s to avoid the arranged marriage that an uncle had planned for him, a move that would have monumental consequences for the future of South Africa.

This intense, often violent, unrest led to new debates in the white community between supporters of fascism and advocates of an expanded democracy. In many respects, the country stood at a crossroads. The Afrikaner nationalist movement, ignited in the 1930s under the leadership of the Broederbond and Malan's Purified National Party, was increasing in strength as the war began. Some 400,000 Afrikaner men who admired Adolf Hitler flocked to the pro-Nazi Ossewabrandwag (oxwagon guard). Smaller numbers who joined its paramilitary subgroup, the Stormtroopers, blew up power lines, post offices, shops, and banks, and beat up Jews and soldiers. Many of those interned as Nazi sympathizers (including future prime minister John Vorster) became prominent politicians when a new government assumed power in 1948.

But at the same time, many white liberals favored an easing of racial discrimination and accepted increasing African urbanization. The 1942 Smit Report on urban Africans, commissioned by Smuts's government, reflected this position. Its authors strongly condemned state-sponsored policies of segregation and advocated an end to the pass laws and improvements in black wages and working conditions. Amid fears of growing juvenile delinquency in the cities and the breakdown of family life, liberal policy makers and missionaries initiated new social programs, including community centers that were designed, in the earlier words of American urban missionary Ray Phillips, to provide "clean, wholesome, and character building"[4] leisure activities for adults and children.

Adding to the tension, African workers and young people were also growing more militant. Illustrating both the potential power and the vulnerability of the trade union movement was the devastating mineworkers' strike in 1946. Founded in 1941 by communist ANC members, the African Mineworkers' Union (AMU) grew steadily during the war. Despite its numbers, the Chamber of Mines and the government consistently rejected workers' demands for regular wage increases, an end to the system of housing workers in cramped compounds, and union recognition. In 1946, distressed with their negligible progress, union officials called for a steep increase in the minimum wage to ten shillings a day, threatening to strike if this demand was not met. On August 12, 1946, between sixty thousand and seventy thousand miners refused to go down into the pits. Police surrounded the mining compounds, arrested union leaders, and brutally attacked the strikers, leaving twelve men dead and twelve hundred wounded. Although the failure of this action destroyed the AMU, its confrontational legacy contributed to the wave of political consciousness that was arising among a new generation of young people.

Under the leadership of A. B. Xuma in the 1940s, the ANC began to respond to growing African militancy by strengthening existing branches and organizing new ones. At the urging of Madie Hall, his newly arrived African American wife, women were admitted as members for the first time in 1943. During Xuma's term as ANC president, from 1940 to 1949, he urged all South Africans to join in the fight for freedom. "The time has now come," he wrote, "that all self-respecting Africans—men & women must join in the struggle for their own liberation. All liberty loving people, men and women of good-will of [all] races must join in this struggle."[5]

Dedicated as Xuma was to black advancement and equality, South Africa was changing rapidly in ways that tested the polite gradualism and mild exhortations of his generation and prompted the formation of new political groups. Younger men such as Walter Sisulu, Nelson Mandela, Anton Lembede, A. P. Mda, and Oliver Tambo, more closely attuned to the upsurge of popular protest around them, began to reject the moderate stance of their elders in the ANC and in 1943 formed the Youth League to hammer out new means of confronting oppression. Among the group's first acts was to issue the Youth League Manifesto that criticized the ANC as representing only the most privileged members of the community, concerned mainly to preserve elite rights. In tune with the ideologies of liberation surging across the colonized world in the mid-1940s, the manifesto emphasized that the group must be "the brains-trust and power-station of the spirit of African nationalism; the spirit of African self-determination."[6] According to this perspective, which they termed Africanism, many members of the ANC Youth League believed that "No foreigner can ever be a true and genuine leader of the African people because no foreigner can every [sic] truly and genuinely interpret the African spirit."[7] They also rejected the class analysis of the Communist Party; rather, they argued that Africans, as a conquered race, were oppressed "by virtue of their colour as a race— . . . —as a nation!"[8] not as a class. Though Lembede, the movement's chief theorist and first president, died prematurely in 1947, Mandela and Tambo went on to dedicate their legal expertise to the struggle for liberation. Also in 1943, a group of Trotskyists formed the Non-European Unity Movement (NEUM), which drew together coloured activists in Cape Town opposed to the formation of a separate Coloured Affairs Department and eastern Cape members of the All African Convention. Their main tactic was noncollaboration with any government bodies.

More important than the Youth League's analysis of race and class, however, was its political strategy. Inspired by the popular protests going on in the cities, League members believed that the dispossessed urban population could be mobilized in support of African nationalism through mass action, including boycotts, strikes, and civil disobedience. One statement clearly articulated this philosophy: "Every Youth Leaguer must go down to the masses. Brush aside all liberals—both white and black. No compromise is our motto. We recognise only one authority—the people, and our leader can only be he who is with the people."[9]

Tensions between the Youth League and the established ANC continued through the mid-1940s. But the brutal suppression of the mine workers' strike in 1946, followed by the election in 1948 of a white government dedicated to new forms of racial separation, finally convinced the organization's members that the more hostile political environment demanded a bolder, more activist strategic vision. At the annual conference in 1949, the Youth League's "Programme of Action" was adopted as official ANC policy and James Moroka, who supported the Youth League and its call for civil disobedience, replaced Xuma as president.

In preparation for the national elections in 1948, which pitted Smuts and D. F. Malan against each other, a National Party commission produced the Sauer Report, which introduced the term apartheid into the country's political lexicon. The report outlined two possible directions for racial policy. Under the first policy of equality (essentially Cape liberalism), all "civilized and educated" people, regardless of race, would have political rights, including the right to vote. Under apartheid (or "separateness"), by contrast, the state would protect the racial purity of the white population by defining and maintaining other racial groups as "separate national communities." Confined to their own areas, these groups would be able to preserve "national pride, self-respect, and mutual respect among the various races of the country." Clearly favoring separation, the report concluded that equality would lead to "national suicide for the white race."[10] With their platform of apartheid, Afrikaner nationalists captured seventy-nine seats in Parliament (the National Party seventy and the Afrikaner Party nine). The opposition United Party won sixty-five seats and the Labour Party six, in a franchise system weighted toward the rural areas. Although succeeding governments reshaped their programs over time in response to both internal and external changes and challenges, the National Party, with apartheid as its guiding principle, held power until 1994.

The legislation that put apartheid into effect was implemented piecemeal beginning in the late 1940s. The new laws built on the country's legacy of racial segregation and white supremacy, strengthening existing regulations and adding new ones. In this process, older patterns of segregation were transformed into a complex system for controlling the labor and movement of Africans and clearly defining and separating the country's four officially designated racial groups—Africans, coloureds, Asians, and whites. To the extent possible, the boundaries between African ethnic communities were sharpened. From 1960 through the 1980s, National Party leaders continued to adapt apartheid policies and regulations with each succeeding crisis, particularly those associated with Sharpeville in 1960 and Soweto in 1976.

The word apartheid continues to evoke countless disturbing images: demolition workers razing houses in Johannesburg's Sophiatown and Cape Town's District Six to clear prime urban property for whites; trucks dumping black families and their possessions onto empty, barren grounds in the countryside lacking water or sanitation; a screaming young student cradling the body of Hector Peterson, shot by police during the Soweto uprising of 1976; and prime ministers Hendrik Verwoerd and P. W. Botha angrily declaring their intention to hold the line against "communist" agitators.

These dramatic images reflect the brutality and violence inherent in implementing and enforcing this racist system, which was premised on a strict classification and regulation of the entire population. Under the Population Registration Act, each person was categorized by race. Whereas in the past, with more loosely defined categories, many coloureds were able to pass as whites, the Race Classification Board was now empowered to rule on "borderline" cases. Indeed, the government became so intent on drawing precise lines among people from different racial groups that officials were forced to devise extraordinary new ways to test these designations. Whether a pencil held fast in someone's hair became a critical factor in defining the often-ambiguous boundaries between "Africans" and "coloureds." Backing up this stricter classification system, new "immorality" laws forbade all sexual relationships between whites and

Beginning in 1955, the apartheid government began the forced removal of the 65,000 residents of Sophiatown, the lively center of black political and cultural life in Johannesburg, which was located in an area designated for whites. Residents' homes were razed and their possessions loaded onto trucks and dumped in Meadowlands and other segregated townships far from the city center. UWC-Robben Island Mayibuye Archives.

nonwhites, and the pass laws were tightened and more strictly enforced. No African man could obtain or switch employment without the proper signatures on his pass book, and authorities began making plans to force African women to carry passes as well.

These measures were intended to push back the tide of African urbanization from its wartime peak, when black families flooded into the cities in record numbers, causing a critical housing shortage in Johannesburg. Rather than adopting liberal reforms to address the resulting dislocation, apartheid measures sought to restrict residence in the cities to men whose labor was needed by white employers and to implement strict controls on the movement of women and children from rural areas. Reflecting the state's dehumanization of African women, one official called them "superfluous appendages" of their husbands and fathers. The new regulations made it almost impossible for a woman to remain in a city unless she had been born there or had worked for a single employer for a lengthy period of time. Without such rights, she could obtain a visitor's pass for seventy-two hours but then had to return to her rural home.

Having provided for the strict division of the population along racial lines, the architects of apartheid passed the Group Areas Act as the blueprint for complete spatial segregation in the cities between people classified by race. With all areas designated for a particular "racial group," anyone else living there had to leave voluntarily or risk being forcibly evicted by the police. Africans uprooted from their neighborhoods were resettled in bleak, dusty townships where they could no longer own their own land or homes. In the countryside, the former reserves were divided into separate territories, at first called Bantustans (using a term for African people now considered outdated and derogatory) and later renamed Homelands. These areas became the dumping grounds for more than three and a half million blacks, uprooted against their will by a state determined to implement its plans for racial and ethnic separation.

The philosophy of apartheid also extended into education. Though mission schools had offered a rigorous academic curriculum, equal to that of many white institutions, these schools were increasingly unable to meet the needs of the growing numbers of urban Africans. By the 1950s, many were severely overcrowded, operating with insufficient funds and underqualified teachers. In the government's eyes, they were also subversive, teaching dangerous liberal ideas and turning students into "imitation" Westerners. To provide basic mass schooling for working-class children in an increasingly segregated society, the Minister of Native Affairs, Hendrik Verwoerd, established a restructured, government-controlled system of "Bantu education" aimed at reinforcing ethnic identities and lowering student aspirations. "What is the use," he argued, "of teaching a Bantu [African] child mathematics when it [sic] cannot use it in practice?"[11] In line with this vision of a separate and subordinate educational system, schools were ordered to use African languages such as Zulu, Xhosa, and Sotho in the lower primary grades, making English and Afrikaans compulsory only for older students. Whereas, in the past, the major universities had accepted small numbers of black students, segregated institutions of higher education were now planned for each racial and ethnic group, with much lower standards than in the white universities. During the late 1960s, these African institutions would become critical centers of antiapartheid struggle.

Recognizing the likelihood of resistance to these policies, the government passed the Suppression of Communism Act in 1950, which defined "communism" so broadly that it included any form of opposition to official policy. Targeting not only political organizations, but also trade union activity, books and magazines, and any other potential source of criticism, the state could now ban groups, publications, and individuals by ministerial decree. Among the law's first victims were influential trade unionists such as Solly Sachs, whose success in organizing both Afrikaner and black garment workers had aroused right-wing anger, and Ray Alexander, a tireless advocate of nonracial unionism among food and canning workers. Under these orders, individuals were restricted to a particular district, had to report regularly to the police, and were prevented from associating with more than one person at a time. They could not be quoted in the press or in any other publication and were prohibited from taking part in political or union organization. Between 1952 and 1955, more than fifty union officials were banned.

Beginning on June 26, 1952, after the government refused to comply with an ANC ultimatum demanding the repeal of apartheid legislation, hundreds of local protests across the country put the Youth League philosophy of nonviolent confrontation into action. In Boksburg, Walter Sisulu and fifty others were arrested when, backed by crowds of supporters, they walked through the gates of this segregated township without the appropriate permits. In the coastal city of Port Elizabeth, thirty people marched through the European-only entrance to the railway station singing freedom songs. Accompanied by cheering friends and family, they chanted "Mayibuye Afrika!" (Let Africa come back!). On the same night, Nelson Mandela and his law partner Oliver Tambo emerged at midnight from a meeting and were arrested for breaking the curfew laws in central Johannesburg. Mandela recalled, "I felt like explaining to him [the police officer] that I was in charge of running the campaign . . . and was not scheduled to defy and be arrested until much later, but of course, that would have been ridiculous."[12]

These widespread protests, particularly strong in the eastern Cape, launched the Defiance Campaign, the first major nationwide program of civil disobedience aimed at challenging the apartheid regime. In support of the tightly organized groups that deliberately violated laws mandating segregated facilities and residential areas, crowds of exuberant supporters gathered in mass meetings and demonstrations, carrying banners and chanting protest slogans. Mandela remembered the high spirits of the protesters. "Even on the way to prison, the vans swayed to the rich voices of the defiers singing *Nkosi Sikelel' iAfrika*" (God Bless Africa), the hauntingly beautiful African national anthem."[13] Following the tradition of nonviolent resistance pioneered by South Africa's

Indian community, those defying the law in support of democratic reform voluntarily courted arrest and prison sentences (usually two to three months) rather than pay fines.

The Defiance Campaign transformed the ANC into a mass movement. By the end of 1952, membership climbed to 100,000 people and the number of branches rose from fourteen to eighty-seven. To sustain this growth in membership, the organization drafted the "M Plan," Nelson Mandela's strategy for organizing local, grassroots ANC cells throughout the country. Although the inability to pay more than a few full-time organizers hindered the plan's implementation, leaders such as Albert Luthuli, the Methodist lay preacher who was elected president of the ANC in 1952, expressed optimism about the possibility for South Africa's peaceful conversion to a democratic, multiracial society. Like many other ANC leaders at the time, he believed that whites would change if they fully understood the absurdities and injustices of the system. In his presidential address to the ANC Annual Conference in 1953, Chief Luthuli strongly condemned the inhumanity of apartheid legislation, calling on his listeners to "keep up the spirit of defiance and thus keep ourselves in readiness for any call to service in the interest of our liberatory movement."[14] While reiterating the ANC commitment to nonviolence, he hoped that "the powers that be" would "make it possible for us to keep our people in this mood."[15]

By welcoming cooperation with local groups of the South African Indian Congress, the Defiance Campaign represented a shift from the Africanist position of the early Youth League, which held that Africans alone should carry out the struggle. With the implementation of apartheid, many ANC activists came to believe that interracial cooperation was necessary to intensify pressure on the government and to build a stronger antiapartheid movement. Furthermore, the race riots in Durban in 1949, in which fifty Indians and eighty-seven Africans were killed and countless others died from injuries, had alarmed leaders of both groups; as a result they recognized the urgent need to form an alliance against a government whose policies would further divide their communities. When the Defiance Campaign led only to stricter laws against protests rather than to constructive change, a broader coalition of organizations, now including the South African Coloured People's Organization and the newly formed white Congress of Democrats (COD), came together as the Congress Alliance. Meeting in June 1955 near Kliptown outside Johannesburg, the three thousand delegates adopted the Freedom Charter, a document that formed the basis of ANC political philosophy into the 1990s. Declaring in the first line, "South Africa belongs to all who live in it, black and white," and promising equality for "all national groups," the Charter established important fundamental principles for a more egalitarian state.

Influenced by the communist background of some delegates, the document also supported a democratic socialist program in which mines, banks, and industry would belong to "the people as a whole" and land would be divided "among those who work it."[16] While envisioning a society that could not have come about without significant structural transformation, most Congress leaders still believed that nonviolent pressure would lead to significant change. Although the Charter became a core statement for the ANC, the role of the COD, many of whose members were communists, was to become a critical political issue.

By the mid-1950s, the opposition movement had to contend with continual harassment from the state. In 1955, the government banned forty-two ANC members, including key leaders such as Walter Sisulu and Nelson Mandela. A year later, 156 prominent activists were arrested and charged with treason. The trial dragged on for five years, draining the time and energy of the ANC and exhausting the organization's resources. Yet this ordeal also strengthened the commitment and solidarity of the defendants. In the words of one of the accused, women's movement activist Helen Joseph, "We led a life within a life and became ever more firmly bound to our organizations and to our common struggle. The effort to turn us from our path had resulted only in a stronger determination to follow it, as almost the whole of the Congress leadership . . . sat together, discussed together, planned together for the future."[17]

Despite intense repression, the incidence of protest activities continued to soar in these years. Parents organized freedom schools to fight against Bantu education; a group of outspoken white women formed the Black Sash to campaign against the abolition of the coloured vote, which Parliament finally passed in 1956; communities scheduled for destruction as "black spots" rallied to prevent their demolition; and women and workers launched new organizations to protest the injustices of apartheid. In 1955, as the government prepared to raze Sophiatown, ANC leaders mounted a spirited campaign to persuade both owners and tenants to "defend your homes to the bitterest ends, to the last ditch."[18] During the same period, the trade union movement was organizing its own protests against new regulations that forbade established unions from including African members. SACTU (the South African Congress of Trade Unions), the new multiracial federation formed in 1955 in defiance of apartheid laws, campaigned aggressively to raise

The struggle against the pass laws, which included demonstrations, strikes, boycotts, and petitions, was a cornerstone of anti-apartheid organizing during the 1950s and early 1960s. As part of these protests, Nelson Mandela burned his pass in 1959. Eli Weinberg, UWC-Robben Island Mayibuye Archives.

the minimum wage and organized a potato boycott that won some improvements in the brutal conditions of farm workers.

Threatened with the prospect of being forced to carry passes, women played a vital part in these campaigns. Resisting official efforts at intimidation, on August 9, 1956, 20,000 women gathered peacefully outside the government office buildings in Pretoria, carrying thousands of petitions to the prime minister, Johannes Strijdom. When he refused to see the women's representatives, they stacked the petitions outside his office door and marched back to the expansive plaza overlooking the city. The demonstrators, many with babies on their backs, stood silently

Police attacking women protesters at Cato Manor near Durban in 1959. Women had stormed municipal beer halls, chased out customers, and destroyed the beer in protest against stepped-up police raids on illegal brewing, which provided many women with their major source of income. UWC-Robben Island Mayibuye Archives.

for thirty minutes and then burst into the song that became emblematic of their movement: "Strijdom, you have tampered with the women, You have struck a rock."[19]

This historic gathering represented the efforts of the Federation of South African Women, formed in 1954 by a multiracial group closely tied to the ANC and the Congress Alliance. Leaders Lilian Ngoyi, Frances Baard, Ray Alexander, and Helen Joseph emphasized women's common bond as mothers and castigated apartheid policies for separating migrant workers from their families. Conveying this perspective most dramatically, Lilian Ngoyi thundered in a speech, "My womb is shaken when they speak of Bantu education."[20] After the Pretoria demonstration the Federation planned a massive campaign of civil disobedience in which women would refuse to take out passes, going to prison if necessary to make their point. Although the ANC leadership weighed in against this plan, women's unrest continued to spread, both in the cities and in rural areas, where women rallied, sometimes violently, against both passes and schemes to "improve" rural economies.

The most explosive rural protests occurred in Eastern Pondoland in the Transkei, an area where the apartheid government had chosen the unpopular Paramount Chief Botha Sigcau to introduce the Bantu Authorities system. As anger and frustration mounted and popular unrest grew in March 1960, the government refused requests to hear people's grievances, which also included Bantu education and tax increases. On June 6, when a group of Africans met to discuss their complaints, police ignored the white flag the protesters had raised and fired into the crowd without warning, killing eleven people.

The unrest in Pondoland coincided with another series of fateful confrontations. In 1959, after a series of heated conflicts within the Transvaal branch of the ANC, a small group of men, among them Robert Sobukwe, a lecturer in African languages at the University of the Witwatersrand, and Potlako Leballo, a teacher dismissed during the Defiance Campaign, split off to form a new organization, the Pan Africanist Congress (PAC). The division reflected lingering Africanist sentiments within the ANC as its leaders developed closer ties with progressives of all racial backgrounds. Like the Youth League members a decade earlier, they believed that Africans should carry out the struggle on their own. Raised in Afrikaner areas, many of the PAC founders had had few social contacts with whites. They objected to the multiracialism of the Congress Alliance and favored a return to the strong Africanist position articulated earlier in the Youth League's Programme of Action by which Africans would organize independently of other racial groups. Reflecting this perspective, one member, challenging the influence of ideas from the outlawed Communist party, explained, "The masses do not hate an abstraction like 'oppression' or 'capitalism.' . . . They make these things concrete and hate the oppressor—in South Africa the white man."[21]

After several months of trying to forge a distinct protest strategy, the PAC leaders decided to stage a mass action against the pass laws in which all African men would leave their passes at home and present themselves for arrest at the local police station. The PAC's charismatic leader Robert Sobukwe assumed that if everyone stayed home from work, the economy would be paralyzed and a spontaneous mass uprising and prolonged general strike would follow. On March 21, 1960, some five thousand people began gathering early in the morning outside the police station at Sharpeville, thirty-five miles south of Johannesburg, where organizing efforts had been particularly successful. Police hovered overhead in low-flying military planes to intimidate the crowd. In the early afternoon, when a scuffle broke out at the gate to the station, people began to push forward. Police claimed they had ordered everyone to leave the area, but few heard the command. Alleging that stones were being thrown at them, officers opened fire. *Drum* magazine reporter Humphrey Tyler offered a widely quoted eyewitness account: "Before the shooting, I heard no warning to the crowd to disperse. There was no warning volley. When the shooting started it did not stop until there was no living thing in the huge compound in front of the police station. The police have claimed they were in desperate danger because the crowd was stoning them. Yet only three policemen were reported to have been hit by stones—and more than 200 Africans were shot down."[22] The majority of the dead were shot in the back while fleeing from the police.

Alarmed reaction to Sharpeville and to subsequent massive protests in Cape Town set in motion dramatic local reactions and an international outcry. The government responded with increased repression; both the ANC and the PAC were banned on April 8, and by May eighteen thousand people had been arrested. The banning, which would remain in place for nearly thirty years, followed a peaceful demonstration of thirty thousand people in Cape Town on March 31. Led by university student Philip Ngosana, this spontaneous response to arrests and shootings earlier that morning provoked fears of a major uprising. Prime Minister Hendrik Verwoerd took an unrelenting stand, proclaiming in Parliament: "We will see to it that we remain in power in this white South Africa."[23] The international community responded to these events with alarm. The South African economy plummeted as foreign investors feared that the country would unravel, and the United Nations Security Council passed a resolution (over British and French abstentions) that called on South Africa to end apartheid.

At this point, despairing of achieving their goals through continued nonviolent action, leading political activists, including members of the ANC and the PAC, turned to more revolutionary strategies and began organizing underground. Key members also left South Africa to learn from the experience of anticolonial struggles elsewhere in Africa and to rally support throughout the continent. Oliver Tambo escaped across the border into Botswana (then Bechuanaland) to set up an external ANC mission, while Nelson Mandela, in disguise and constantly moving around to escape the authorities, became the chief spokesperson for the ANC. Dubbed the "Black Pimpernel" by the press, he also slipped out of the country, garnering support for the ANC in independent African countries, studying guerrilla warfare in Algeria (which had just won independence from France after eight years of armed struggle), and arranging military training and educational programs for young ANC members. In this tense and difficult period, the ANC created Umkhonto we Sizwe (Spear of the Nation, also known as MK). A small, tightly knit group, MK included some committed white allies and advocated a carefully controlled campaign of sabotage, but took care not to kill or injure people. Lilliesleaf Farm in Rivonia, nineteen miles north of Johannesburg, became their secret headquarters. Within eighteen months, the group took responsibility for more than two hundred attacks on targets such as government buildings, post offices, and railway installations and equipment, and sent some three hundred men to China, the Soviet Union, and other African countries for military instruction.

Other groups also opted for violent resistance. Shortly before the MK campaign, a small group of people, mainly white, with varied political backgrounds, formed the African Resistance Movement. Relying on dynamite and electrical timing mechanisms, they blew up dams, power lines, and railway signaling systems. Poqo, founded by the PAC, took its name from a Xhosa word meaning "alone" or "pure." With strong support in the Cape, Poqo members envisioned a spontaneous mass uprising that would sweep away the apartheid regime. A recruiting message from 1961 proclaimed triumphantly: "Africa will be free on January 1st. The white people shall suffer, the black people will rule. Freedom comes after bloodshed."[24] In preparation for this uprising, they assassinated policemen, suspected informers, chiefs, and random whites.

This turn to violence produced a fierce government reaction. During 1962 and 1963 the leaders of these groups were arrested, largely through information from informers within the movement, and perhaps from an American CIA agent in Durban. At the famous Rivonia trial from November 1963 until June 1964, named after the Johannesburg suburb where the ANC accused had been taken into custody, the defendants, including Walter Sisulu, were sentenced to life imprisonment, narrowly missing the death sentences they had expected. PAC leader Robert Sobukwe, apprehended after Sharpeville, remained in prison until 1969. The ARM members who had not fled the country received jail terms of up to fifteen years. In his defense at the Rivonia trial, Nelson Mandela eloquently defended ANC actions, recounting the birth of the movement in 1912 and its history of failed efforts to challenge government policies by nonviolent means. He closed his poignant plea for equal rights and democracy by reiterating his "cherished ideal" of a free society in which people of all races live together in harmony with equal opportunities. "It is an ideal which I hope to live for and to achieve. But if need be, it is an ideal for which I am prepared to die."[25]

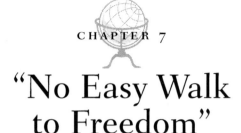

CHAPTER 7

"No Easy Walk to Freedom"

Just as South Africa was intensifying racial exploitation in the late 1940s and 1950s, other countries throughout the world were successfully casting off the chains of colonialism and racial domination. During the mid-1950s, when D. F. Malan and Hendrik Verwoerd were taking steps to force women to carry passes, Rosa Parks and Martin Luther King Jr. were boycotting segregated buses, inaugurating massive civil rights protests in the United States. Elsewhere in Africa, nationalist leaders were organizing mass movements and guerrilla struggles that ousted British, French, and Portuguese colonial rulers. This context meant that criticism of apartheid came not only from internal opposition movements, but also from international sources, particularly after the massacre of anti-pass protesters at Sharpeville focused international attention on the brutality necessary to uphold South Africa's racial order.

Yet internally, the National Party maintained an absolute monopoly on power. With Broederbond members firmly in control of the government and Afrikaners dominating the civil service, the United Party could offer only weak opposition. In a referendum held in October 1960, 52 percent of voters opted to leave the British Commonwealth and make South Africa a republic, thereby severing the imperial link with Britain and further isolating the country from external political pressure. Once international investment picked up by the end of 1961, South Africa resumed its postwar economic expansion, making its white population among the most prosperous in the world. As foreign investment soared to new heights, the economy achieved a growth rate of nearly 6 percent a year. Along with economic strength came heightened defense and technical capabilities supplied by new trading arrangements with West Germany and France, which edged out Britain and the United States as the country's primary economic partners. By 1980, South Africa was well equipped with helicopters, Mirage fighter-bombers, and other military technology and had launched efforts to develop a nuclear capability. Meanwhile ARMSCOR, a government-controlled corporation, began manufacturing its own weapons both for export and for internal use.

In this expansive economic climate, the National Party continued to consolidate the power it had gained in 1948. Hendrik Verwoerd, who became prime minister in 1958, had distinct ideas about racial segregation. With a doctorate in psychology from Stellenbosch University, he had studied in Germany during the 1920s, edited *Die Transvaler*, a newspaper accused of transmitting pro-German propaganda during World War II, and in 1950 became the Minister of Native Affairs responsible for implementing forced removals and Bantu education. After surviving one attempt on his life, by a white farmer who proclaimed his "violent urge to shoot at apartheid,"[1] Verwoerd was assassinated in 1966 by a parliamentary messenger who was declared insane and committed to a mental hospital. Verwoerd's successor, B. J. Vorster, prime minister from 1966 to 1978, continued to implement his predecessor's policies of Separate Development.

Under this plan, the scattered rural "Bantustans" of the 1950s were rechristened as "homelands" and offered the option of becoming separate nations, ostensibly independent of white rule from Pretoria. According to the Bantu Homelands Citizenship Act of 1970, all Africans were required to become citizens of one of these territories, losing any claim to citizenship in the larger South African nation. Only four of the ten newly designated countries chose this option—Bophuthatswana, outside Pretoria, in 1977; the Transkei (1976) and the Ciskei (1981), both in the eastern Cape; and tiny Venda, in the far north near the border with Zimbabwe, in 1979. Seeking to keep people from fleeing these impoverished enclaves, efforts began to decentralize industrial production in order to create new jobs in or adjacent to the homelands—a move particularly important in the eastern Cape after Africans were expelled from the western Cape to transform the region into a "coloured preference area."

With these measures, the National Party sought to deny that the country was divided between a roughly 70 percent African majority and a ruling white minority of 17 percent. The remaining population was classified as coloured (10 percent) and Asian (3 percent). Instead, the government argued, South Africa was composed of many "distinctive national units," among them the Sotho, Zulu, Tswana, Xhosa, and Ndebele, each of which, according to official publications, might "attain self-government and independence."[2] Yet whites still held title to 87 percent of the country's total land and controlled the economic infrastructure, whereas the

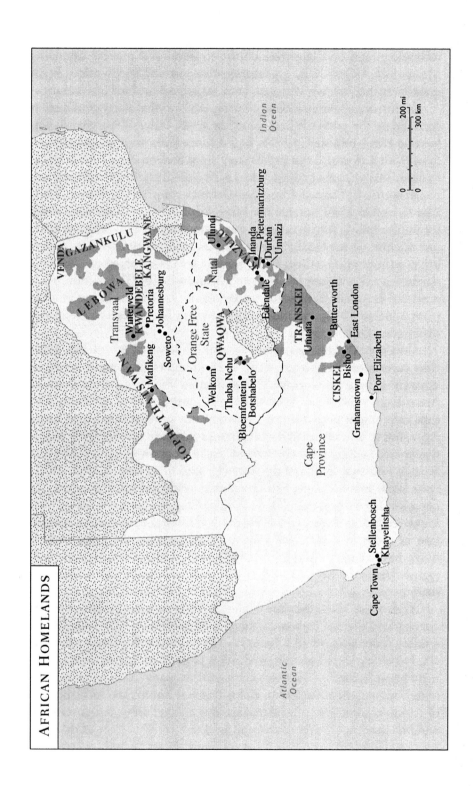

AFRICAN HOMELANDS

Indian
Ocean

200 mi

300 km

VENDA

GAZANKULU

LEBOWA

KWANDEBELE

KANGWANE

Winterveld

Transvaal

Pretoria

Johannesburg

Soweto

Mafikeng

BOPHUTHATSWANA

Orange Free
State

Welkom

Thaba Nchu

Bloemfontein

Botshabelo

QWAQWA

Natal

Umlazi

KWAZULU

Ulundi

Inanda

Pietermaritzburg

Durban

Edendale

TRANSKEI

Butterworth

Umtata

East London

CISKEI

Bisho

Grahamstown

Port Elizabeth

Cape
Province

Stellenbosch

Cape Town

Khayelitsha

Atlantic
Ocean

black areas, primarily rural and desperately poor, housed those whose labor was not needed in the cities—young married women, children, and older people. Furthermore, the "independence" being offered was a sham, creating new political entities under tight South African control and recognized by no other country. Finally, the designated homeland areas were not contiguous stretches of land; Bophuthatswana, for example, was composed of eight scattered territorial enclaves.

Nonetheless, despite inadequate infrastructure and health and educational facilities, unproductive economies, geographic fragmentation, and limited control over their own development, some new leaders in the homelands built on earlier patterns of local representation and authority to take advantage of the new system that promised political power to a few and a transfer of resources from the South African government. Among them was Lucas Mangope, a primary and secondary school teacher who climbed the ladder of positions in the Tswana regional authorities to become chief minister in 1972 and president when Bophuthatswana became independent in 1977. But ongoing unrest among non-Tswana speakers (a third of the population) led to police violence, tight controls on opposition groups, and, in 1988, an army coup. After South African troops put down the rebellion, Mangope was quickly restored to power.

The pattern was similar in the other states that opted for "independence." In the Ciskei, Lennox Sebe, a teacher and territorial authority official who founded the Ciskei National Independence Party, became president for life in 1983. Despite his extensive travels to Europe and Israel to attract investment, the territory remained desperately poor and, as in Bophuthatswana, was held together partly by a ruthless police force. In the Xhosa-speaking Transkei, Mandela's nephew Kaiser Matanzima had a similar career path in local government and as founder of the Transkei National Independence Party. He retained power with the aid of Pretoria but, under pressure from intense political rivalries, resigned the presidency in 1986. The ensuing crisis was resolved two years later when General Bantu Holomisa staged a military coup and shortly thereafter announced his intention to conduct a plebiscite on whether residents of the Transkei wished to be reincorporated into South Africa. The politics of Venda, a one-party state, also rested on brutal police repression to resolve political tensions.

Parliamentary opposition to apartheid remained muted, apart from the maverick voice of Helen Suzman, the lone representative of the Progressive Party between 1961 and 1974. From the 1950s into the mid-1970s, the United Party retained between a quarter and a third of the seats in the House of Assembly, but was cautious in its criticism of apartheid.

When the party opposed any further transfer of land to the African reserves, eleven of its fifty-three MPs split off in 1959 to form the Progressive Party. For thirteen years, Suzman, a former lecturer in economic history who represented the Johannesburg area of Houghton, was the only member to win an election. The new party adopted a complex plan for a multiracial parliament and Suzman often was the only member of the Assembly to oppose government policies and support human rights. She spoke out against abuses of prisoners held under the ninety-day detention law imposed after Sharpeville and cast the sole vote against the Terrorism Act of 1967, which gave the minister of justice the power to detain people indefinitely and hold them in solitary confinement for purposes of interrogation. She also lambasted the government for the plight of those forcibly removed to the homelands. Speaking in Parliament she decried, "People have been put on the veld, some of them in midwinter, and given tents which they probably did not even know how to erect; they were left there with no proper medical attention, no proper facilities for schooling and no proper store facilities for obtaining necessities."[3] After Suzman was reelected in 1966, the *New York Times* wrote, "There is basis for believing that as the sole voice of the voteless, she actually represents more South Africans than all the other members of Parliament combined."[4]

Just as government policy worked against the tide of international opinion in reinforcing racial domination, it also attempted to counter the tendency of many urban Africans to reject "tradition" and "tribalism" and to embrace ideas and practices associated with modernity. The iconoclastic *Drum* magazine, published in Johannesburg, both embodied and shaped this trend. Its talented staff of African writers, rooted in the creative literary and musical world of Sophiatown, projected powerful images of the "new" men and women who were emerging as black role models in South Africa's cities. The magazine highlighted black achievement, especially in music and sports, also attracting readers with scantily clad "cover girls," advertisements for the latest African American hair straightening and skin lightening products, muckraking exposés of brutal conditions in prisons and on potato farms, and celebrations of the illicit life of *tsotsis*, youth gangsters, and *shebeens* (illegal drinking clubs). Even when its content was not overtly political, *Drum* celebrated a world of black talent and sophistication that the apartheid state sought to extinguish.

Gifted and creative South African musicians also reflected this modernizing impulse. Inspired by American jazz, groups such as the Jazz Maniacs and the Alexandra All-Star Band pioneered *kwela* and *mbaqanga,* lively new musical forms rooted in working-class township life and local melodic and rhythmic idioms. Kwela music, which developed during the 1940s and 1950s, relied on the pennywhistle, an inexpensive tin flute, for its lead voice and repeating melodies; *mbaqanga,* popular as dance music among vocal groups such as the Manhattan Brothers, combined guitar and brass instruments. Singer Dolly Rathebe was hailed as the South African Billie Holiday after starring in the British-produced film, "Jim Comes to Jo'burg," the first sympathetic movie portrayal of the lives of urban Africans. When prominent musicians such as singer Miriam Makeba, trumpet player Hugh Masekela, and pianist Dollar Brand (later Abdullah Ibrahim) fled the country in the early 1960s, South Africa's distinct blend of harmony and rhythm found enthusiastic international audiences.

Similar to these musicians, with their eclectic styles, some distinguished writers engaged the relationship between modernity and tradition by continuing the country's literary heritage in African languages. Following in the path of Xhosa scholar A. C. Jordan and of poets who wrote in Xhosa, Zulu, and Sotho, Mazisi Kunene produced two major epic poems, *Emperor Shaka the Great,* which challenged European accounts of the influential ruler, and *Anthem of the Decades,* recounting the Zulu version of creation. He also wrote two anthologies of Zulu poems, a master's thesis that surveys the entire history of Zulu poetry, and numerous unpublished poems and epics. Like the Kenyan writer Ngugi wa Thiong'o, Kunene was dedicated to ending what he considered the poisonous colonial legacy of African literature in European languages. In a tribute to Magolwane, the great Zulu poet of the early nineteenth century, he wrote:

> After the festival, after the feast
> After the singing
> After the voices have faded into the night
> And the sounds of talking have ceased
> And the angry winds have shed their manes
> And people have stopped to dance
> Your voice and your voice only
> Shall rise from the ruins.[5]

The vibrant culture of Sophiatown always faced the threat of extinction from a state determined to wipe out any vestiges of spontaneity in black urban society. In 1955 the government began to expel its residents to the endless rows of tiny, uniform "matchbox houses" of Soweto, far from the center of Johannesburg, where tenants were issued ninety-nine-year leases but could never own their own homes. A decade later, bulldozers razed the coloured community of District Six in Cape Town, forcing its residents into equally bleak new townships on the harsh, sandy Cape Flats.

Meanwhile rural life grew increasingly grim, both for those who had never left and for people forcibly driven from areas designated as "black spots." The latter were often dumped unceremoniously on barren land equipped only with latrines and communal water taps on which they might build corrugated tin houses and try to reconstruct their lives. People forcibly removed to the tiny KwaNdebele "homeland" described the process as a kind of natural disaster that "scoops you up when you least expect it and drops you somewhere you have never seen, leaving it to you to patch together the torn and ragged pattern of a life."[6] Others expressed more overt anger; Jim Masetlana, a former tenant on a white farm who had been uprooted three times, explained: "This is no homeland, . . . Where I grew up was really a homeland. I had land. I could plow. Even the white farmers give you land to plow. This type of homeland I have never seen. They have no business taking us from the place of our birth."[7]

New York Times reporter Joseph Lelyveld wrote that he had thought he grasped the meaning of the statistics—that within the twenty years from 1960 to 1980 the black population living in the "homelands" had zoomed from 39.8 percent to 53.1 percent—until he confronted the "visual shock" of their significance in the "closer settlements" outside Pretoria. There he found a sea of "metal shanties and mud houses the metal roofs of which were typically weighted down by small boulders to keep them from blowing off in the Transvaal's violent hailstorms. Such sights can be seen in other countries," he wrote, "usually as a result of famines or wars. I don't know where else they have been achieved as a result of planning."[8]

Throughout the countryside, the women, children, and older people who were left behind struggled to farm on increasingly barren land, often trudging miles each day to fetch water from drying streams and subsisting on irregular remittances from family members working in the mines or cities. In some rural communities, disease and starvation were so common that half the children died before reaching the age of five years. At Dimbaza, a resettlement community in the Ciskei, ninety graves were dug within six months of its establishment, seventy of them for children.

Under apartheid, the African churches that had staked out their autonomy against European missionaries now thrived in their own separate worlds. While Methodism and other recognized denominations retained their attraction for middle-class blacks, and women continued to gather each Thursday with their *manyano* (women's union) groups, the number of African-run churches rose from eight hundred to twenty-two hundred between 1948 and 1960. Although the beliefs and practices of their adherents initially had reflected resistance to white control, in the 1950s there was a tendency toward accommodation with white society as major church leaders such as Isaiah Shembe and John Masowe built successful business enterprises and more chiefs became members of leading African-initiated churches. Having created their own thriving communities apart from the white churches, some leaders shared the apolitical, uncritical sentiments of the head of the government-recognized African Congregational Church, who explained: "I like the Nationalist government. And I tell my people, don't take any interest in this colour bar. Forget about it, forget about politics!"[9]

As these churches became stronger and more self-confident, some of them also grew less adamant in their cultural resistance. Having overcome their initial opposition to Western influence, more church members now sent their children to government-run primary schools than in the past and many adherents of these congregations allowed their followers to seek western medical care. Charismatic Zionist groups remained suspicious of secondary education, however, and their prophets, usually avid healers themselves, sometimes met discharged patients at the hospital for a ceremony to counter the effects of Western medical treatment. Reflecting the spiritual aspects of their separatist sentiments, many priests continued to condemn the portrayal of Jesus in white churches. A revivalist preacher proclaimed in his sermon: "God is a good God. But he is not a European. Anyone who says that is a fool. Jesus has never set foot on the soil of Europe or America or Australia. But—Jesus has been in Africa."[10]

The contrast between the lives of most blacks and whites could not have been more stark. In the words of South African-born author Lewis DeSoto, "Through it all we lived in our comfortable houses with our gardens, our swimming pools, our holidays at the seaside resorts—and our servants. . . . We lived like strangers, in a strange land."[11] Although not all whites were equally prosperous, those in the cities and towns (80 percent of whites by the 1950s) inhabited a cosmopolitan world similar to that in Europe and America, although the cramped, dank quarters of black servants ubiquitous in suburban backyards belied the government intent of total separation. "Johannesburg lay in Africa," in the words of journalist Rian Malan, "but that was more or less incidental." With "skyscrapers, smart department stores, cinemas, and theaters. It was part of a larger world. There was no TV in my boyhood. . . . We had radio, though, and all the characters in the boys' serials were British or American."[12]

In the context of postwar prosperity and expanded higher education, the lives and even the politics of English and Afrikaans speakers became more similar. As more Afrikaner men moved out of agriculture and factory work into professional fields and civil service employment and as women entered nursing, teaching, and clerical and sales jobs, their per capita income began to approach that of the English. Communities of suburban houses and lawns expanded, as did national supermarket chains such as Pick and Pay. Although the Dutch Reformed Church and racial ideology continued to anchor Afrikaner life, tennis and golf also became popular leisure activities as they were in British communities. And both groups embraced rugby, newly popular as the embodiment of masculine competitive prowess. In the general election of 1966, a significant number of English-speaking whites voted for the National Party for the first time. Sheltered from the townships by segregated housing and laws that required whites to obtain a permit in order to enter black communities, most whites rarely encountered the squalor to which apartheid relegated the majority of the country's population.

Yet even at the height of apartheid, Afrikaner attitudes were not monolithic. In 1957, the distinguished Afrikaner poet Van Wyk Louw wrote, "Among the greatest enemies of our volk are those . . . who wish to impose their own narrow vision for this time and eternity."[13] A decade later, Willem de Klerk, whose brother would become president in 1989, contrasted three tendencies in the nationalist movement: the *verligtes* (enlightened ones), liberals who preferred openness and freedom, even in race relations; the *verkramptes* (narrow reactionaries), who clung to the past; and those who represented a "positive Afrikanerhood" that combined the best of these two positions. Reflecting the more enlightened position, a new generation of Afrikaner writers emerged known as the Generation of the Sixties. Most prominent among them were Etienne le Roux, André Brink, and Breyten Breytenbach, whose works nurtured new views of Afrikaner history and culture by exploring themes such as secularism, racial understanding, and sexuality. Most controversial among them was Breytenbach who moved to Paris while in his early twenties, married a Vietnamese woman, and became a French citizen. He also openly condemned apartheid, writing in a letter to the newspaper *Die Burger*, "If I could renounce my being an Afrikaner I would do it. I am ashamed of my people."[14]

From many perspectives, the 1960s looked bleak indeed for black South Africans. The apartheid state had succeeded in destroying the overt resistance movement within the country, imprisoning many key leaders for life and forcing others into exile. As Nelson Mandela relates in his autobiography, the prisoners on Robben Island spent their days in blinding sunlight digging rocks in an open quarry. Later reflecting on this experience he wrote: "I was now on the sidelines, but I also knew that I would not give up the fight. . . . We regarded the struggle in prison as a microcosm of the struggle as a whole. We would fight inside as we had fought outside. The racism and repression were the same; I would simply have to fight on different terms."[15] Having escaped to London, Mandela's former law partner Oliver Tambo worked with others who had fled the country to reestablish the African National Congress (ANC) abroad. Tanzania, housing four guerrilla training camps for Umkhonto we Sizwe (MK) during the 1960s, became its main center of operations and the site from which the ANC launched an unsuccessful effort to aid nationalist fighters in white-ruled Zimbabwe. The 1969 Morogoro Conference, at which the movement was reorganized and membership was opened to whites for the first time, was held in Tanzania. The Pan Africanist Congress (PAC), which had split from the ANC in 1959, was more turbulent and divided in exile. The group adopted the ancient name of Azania for South Africa in an effort to define an alternative black national identity. Meanwhile, Africans felt the full brunt of apartheid resettlement policies, as the population of the Bantustans increased dramatically whereas that of most urban townships declined. By the end of the decade, however, new political voices were beginning to emerge from an unexpected quarter—the segregated black universities built to provide the educated workforce designed to make Separate Development, the policy of promoting ten independent rural homelands, a reality.

The leader of this effort to revive political opposition, which became known as the Black Consciousness Movement, was Steven Bantu Biko, a student in the black section of the University of Natal medical school. His essays, influenced in part by the Black Power and black theology movements in the United States, emphasized the psychological aspects of white domination, arguing that as a prelude to successful resistance, blacks had to overcome the inferiority complex fostered by a racist government and institutions. In "The Quest for a True Humanity," Biko depicted Black Consciousness as "the realization by the black man of the need to rally together with his brothers around the cause of their oppression—the blackness of their skin" and to understand that "the most potent weapon in the hands of the oppressor is the mind of the oppressed."[16] Following a 1967 convention at Rhodes University, where officials refused to allow black delegates to share social facilities with whites, these students broke with the multiracial National Union of South African Students (NUSAS). Two years later, prompted also by the inferior education in homeland universities, they formed the South African Students Organization (SASO).

Though never a mass political organization, SASO, and its allied off-campus group, the Black People's Convention, initiated hundreds of community projects across the country. By opening health centers and economic cooperatives, teaching basic literacy classes, encouraging cultural activities, and founding a general workers' union, these students intended not simply to provide essential services, but to "conscientise" a grassroots constituency—promoting the message of black pride and self-help. While the Black Consciousness movement, like the PAC, eschewed cooperation with whites, these young activists also challenged apartheid racial categories by redefining the term "black" to include coloureds and Asians, whom they also recognized as victims of government oppression. Perhaps the most enduring legacy of the movement, however, came from its success in spreading beyond the universities into the secondary schools, whose students would soon ignite a rebellion that transformed the country forever.

Just as Black Consciousness beliefs were spreading from the campuses into the community, the long-repressed black working class, whose African members were forbidden to form legal trade unions or to strike, was regaining its voice and its political influence. Early in 1973, following strikes by dockers and bus drivers the previous year, men and women working in Durban factories left their jobs in a mass protest against low wages at a time of rising prices, miserable working conditions, and severe limits on organizing. Within days, the strike had spread rapidly, first in Natal as workers marched from factory to factory broadcasting their defiance, and then throughout the country. By the end of the year, 100,000 laborers had staged illegal strikes. Within less than a decade, the repercussions of these actions had led to far-reaching nationwide changes in the laws governing black workers, allowing them to form legal trade unions for the first time in the country's history. Journalist Allister Sparks had been a prophetic voice in 1972 when he wrote in the *Rand Daily Mail* of new pressure on the South African state from black workers. "It will not be temporary this time but will go on growing irresistibly, slowly at first, then rapidly later. And as it does so the processes of change will begin to move again."[17]

The greatest impact of the Black Consciousness Movement came three years later with the rebellion of thousands of high school students in Soweto. Responding to a government decree that math and social studies be taught not in English but in Afrikaans, fifteen thousand to twenty thousand students, some as young as six or seven years old, gathered early on the cold winter morning of June 16, 1976, to march and rally in protest against this ruling. The placards they carried announced their demands: "If we must do Afrikaans, Vorster [the Prime Minister] must do Zulu," "We Don't Want to Learn the Language of Our Oppressors," and "We Want Equal Education Not Slave Education."[18]

Instead of allowing a peaceful protest, which the students had intended, police intervened. When tear gas failed to disperse the crowd, they opened fire. The besieged students retreated, but then fanned out all across Soweto, stoning cars, building barricades, setting fire to township administration buildings and beer halls, and randomly killing two white men who worked for the West Rand Administration Board. The photo of a terrified young girl running alongside a panicked schoolboy who carried the body of their first victim, thirteen-year-old Hector Peterson, has become the iconic image of this resistance. Whereas the proposed change in language instruction had galvanized the students, they were also declaring their opposition to an educational system that consigned them to cramped, severely underfunded schools with fifty or sixty students to a class and inadequately trained teachers.

During the next few days, high school and university students elsewhere joined in the revolt, continuing the attacks on police patrols and government buildings. Writer and tennis champion Mark Mathabane recalls his schoolmates in Alexandra joining the crowds of protesting students the following day. As they marched, they chanted, "Amandla! Awethu! Amandla! Awethu!" (Power is Ours!).[19] Protests continued for several months, with workers organizing several stay-at-homes during August and September in support of the student rebels. The refusal of Zulu migrant workers in the hostels around Johannesburg to support these work stoppages signaled the early stages of a political division that would deepen and spread during the following decade. Students continued to boycott schools throughout 1976. By the end of the revolt, 575 people had died and at least 2,400 were wounded. But the government surrendered to the student demands and left English intact as the major language of instruction.

Though few students considered themselves revolutionaries, their actions initiated a continuing resistance whose momentum eventually led to the fall of apartheid. In contrast to the aftermath of Sharpeville,

Poster commemorating the student uprising of June 16, 1976, which began as a protest against government plans to mandate the use of Afrikaans in high school instruction and turned into a full-scale revolt when police opened fire on peaceful student demonstrators. South African History Archive.

a generalized government crackdown had become impossible. The level of spontaneous popular anger was too high, and workers, students, and other activists found new and more challenging ways to organize. As Steve Biko later wrote: "Everybody saw this as a deliberate act of oppressive measures to try and calm down the black masses, and everybody was determined equally to say to the police, to say to the government: we shall not be scared by your police, by your dogs, and by your soldiers."[20]

The immediate outcome of the Soweto uprising might have seemed disastrous, however. Biko and other Black Consciousness leaders and political activists were detained within months. The following year, in 1977, Mamphela Ramphele, Biko's close associate, was banished from her home and medical clinic in Port Elizabeth (a key center of Black Consciousness) to the northern Transvaal, where she spent seven years treating impoverished patients in a rural health center. Mandela's wife Winnie was exiled to Brandfort, a deeply conservative small town in the Orange Free State, where the police hounded her constantly. Unlike Nelson Mandela, however, Steve Biko did not survive his ordeal. After being arrested at a roadblock in August 1977, he was imprisoned and badly beaten in Port Elizabeth. Severely injured from repeated blows to his head, Biko was thrown naked into the back of a police Land Rover for an eleven-hour trip to a prison hospital in Pretoria where, according to his lawyer's testimony, he died "a miserable and lonely death on a cold prison floor"[21] on September 12. An inquest verified that he had lesions to the brain caused by his injuries. Describing these events to a National Party meeting, justice minister Jimmy Kruger stunned international public opinion by proclaiming his indifference to Biko's brutal treatment, announcing that the death "leaves me cold."[22]

Despite this repression, the international and national reaction to Soweto helped to launch a new era as momentous as the onset of apartheid itself. In the aftermath of the uprising, support for antiapartheid movements escalated in Europe and the United States, generating new connections between internal resistance and external pressure. Government measures to address the growing turbulence among students and workers produced a new generation of freedom fighters and an increasingly powerful, and legal, black trade union movement. In addition, the belated introduction of television into South Africa in 1976 contributed to connecting the country with the outside world, despite tight state control over the media.

Compounding this internal turmoil, by the late 1970s South Africa also faced severe external challenges. Although most African countries (including the neighboring British enclaves of Lesotho, Botswana, and Swaziland) had gained their independence from colonial rule by the mid-1960s, the rest of southern Africa remained under colonial domination: Namibia (then South West Africa) under South African trusteeship through the United Nations, Mozambique and Angola under Portugal's military dictatorship, and Zimbabwe (then Southern Rhodesia) ruled by the British settlers who, in 1965, had defied world opinion and issued a Unilateral Declaration of Independence. By the mid-1970s, however, under the pressure of region-wide armed struggles, dramatic transformations were underway. Following a democratic revolution in Portugal, Mozambique and Angola became independent in 1975, events that inspired students in Soweto. By 1980, a combination of guerrilla warfare and negotiation had installed an African government in Zimbabwe; but not until 1990 was South Africa ousted from Namibia. Whereas in the 1980s, South Africa helped to ignite and sustain civil wars in both former Portuguese territories, the militantly anticolonial bent of the new rulers throughout southern Africa created a hostile environment for the South African government. Because the country's buffer with independent Africa was gone, these "frontline states" became potential launching grounds for guerrilla activity in South Africa.

Following the killing and arrest of many student leaders in 1976, thousands of other young men and women fled the country, providing Umkhonto we Sizwe with an army of new recruits. By 1978, an estimated four thousand refugees were being trained in other African countries, especially Angola, Libya, and Tanzania. With this influx of new, young guerrilla fighters, attacks within South Africa picked up in the early 1980s. These strikes, aimed at strategic targets such as power plants, police stations, and the country's synthetic-oil refinery, were designed to inspire renewed confidence in the power of the exiled ANC.

In an effort to respond to these increasing pressures as well as to the economic threat from rising oil prices and shortages of skilled labor, the state adopted a new approach in the late 1970s, after minister of defense P. W. Botha became prime minister in 1978. Known as the "Total Strategy," these policies sought to win over moderate, middle-class blacks through a series of political reforms, including the ability to control land in the townships on ninety-nine-year leases, support for black business ownership, and granting greater power to "homeland" rulers in order to cultivate them as allies. Among the first of these measures, the 1979 Wiehahn Commission report recommended granting Africans the right to form legally recognized trade unions for the first time in the country's history, while the Riekert Commission proposed an end to the pass laws. The new strategy contributed to a split in the National Party between those who deemed themselves *verligte* (enlightened) and the hardliners, many of whom followed Cabinet member Andries Treurnicht into the newly formed Conservative Party in 1982.

Although the Wiehahn reforms were intended in part as a form of state control, the number of unionized workers soared in the wake of legalization. By 1985, a million workers had joined the newly launched Congress of South African Trade Unions (COSATU), far more than the 150,000 members the Council of Non-European Trade Unions had been able to muster in the 1940s. Although COSATU's affiliated unions agitated for better wages and working conditions, they were also consciously political—dedicated to overturning apartheid and to empowering people for a democratic future by encouraging active participation in daily union struggles. In some COSATU unions women members pushed for a new definition of gender equity that would include not only equal wages, but an end to sexual harassment and to male domination in the unions and at home. Echoing the black mineworkers' strike of 1946, in August 1987 nearly 300,000 gold and coal miners sustained a strike for three weeks, an action that brought Cyril Ramaphosa, the lawyer who led the National Union of Mineworkers (NUM), into the national spotlight. The following year more than a million workers walked off their jobs in response to calls for strike action.

These reforms notwithstanding, apartheid laws reinforcing the migrant labor system continued to take a heavy toll on black families, making it more and more difficult for wives, husbands, and children to live together in either the cities or the countryside. Spouses might be arrested for living with their families in servants' quarters and women in urban townships faced eviction from their homes and removal to the homelands if their husbands died or deserted them. Furthermore, the acute shortage of lodging in the cities spawned huge settlements of dilapidated shacks and overcrowding in state-owned houses. In 1982, more than 21,000 African families were waiting for accommodation in Soweto alone, and anywhere from six to twenty-nine people might be crammed into these tiny dwellings. Government programs to force more and more urban blacks into single-sex hostels, which excluded both spouses and children, threatened to splinter family life still further. In Alexandra township outside Johannesburg, the prototype for this social experiment, eight hostels were planned, each designed to house twenty-five hundred people. One women's hostel resident poignantly summed up the devastating effects of this system: "If the government had set out to create a society that would consume itself, it couldn't have done better. It has destroyed our family life, left the homelands father-less with mothers struggling to help the remains of their family survive. Either the women must go mad or revolt."[23] Government statistics reflected this wreckage. Whereas in 1980 45.7 percent of white women were married, the figure for African women was 23.3 percent.[24]

In 1983, in another futile effort to uphold this inhumane system, the government created new Indian and coloured parliaments separate from the white parliament and with little power, but designed to convince these two groups (and external critics) that each racial and ethnic community had its own democratic representation. Africans were still considered citizens of the homelands. A new umbrella organization formed to resist this cosmetic change and to urge a general boycott of the elections for the new parliaments, the United Democratic Front (UDF), came to play a central role both in organizing resistance and in working covertly with the leaders of the exiled ANC to undermine the white minority government. Albertina Sisulu, wife of imprisoned leader Walter Sisulu, became one of the UDF's three elected presidents. While unable to identify openly with the ANC, UDF organizers (prominent among them the eloquent Anglican archbishop Desmond Tutu, who won the Nobel Peace Prize in 1984) adopted the Freedom Charter as their guiding document.

Although an explicit alliance with the banned ANC would have opened the UDF to charges of treason, its formation as a coalition of hundreds of organizations across the country was inspired through underground contacts between ANC exiles and activists at home. In late 1978, as part of a general strategic review, an ANC delegation had traveled to Vietnam to study how a small guerrilla army had managed to defeat a country as powerful as the United States. The Vietnamese response, to organize a mass political base, creating an activist, politicized civil society, contributed to the formation of the UDF as a coalition of more than six hundred organizations that drew together students, youth, workers, women, writers, artists, and township-based civic associations. Expressing their particular concerns, they boycotted schools and white shops, encouraged rent strikes, organized child care and rape crisis centers, and staged antiapartheid theater. Adopting the slogan "revolution now, education later," some of the most militant young male "comrades" resorted to violence, attacking police, town councilors, and other officials perceived as apartheid collaborators. In contrast to the multiracialism of the 1950s (which rested on a coalition of organizations defined by "race"), the UDF espoused a nonracial ideology, welcoming everyone willing to take part in the struggle. This strategy countered that of AZAPO (the Azanian People's Organization), the Congress of South African Students, and the Azanian Students' Organization, which carried the still-popular mantle of Black Consciousness into the 1980s.

The leadership in the UDF of Archbishop Desmond Tutu and the Rev. Allan Boesak reflected the critical role of liberation theology in the local and international struggle against apartheid. The South African Council of Churches, which spearheaded this religious assault, used its funds to defend political prisoners and their families, while black clergy members spoke at rallies, briefed reporters, and provided support and guidance to antigovernment protestors. Throughout the turmoil of the 1980s, the scarlet ecclesiastical robes of Archbishop Tutu became a symbol of resistance to racial oppression, as church bodies locally and around the world condemned apartheid. Responding to Boesak's powerful leadership, in 1982 the World Alliance of Reformed Churches adopted a resolution condemning apartheid as a sin and a moral heresy, forcing the most extremist branch of the Dutch Reformed Church to resign from the alliance. At the height of the antiapartheid uprising in 1985, 150 clergy of all races and denominations condemned the god of the South African government as "not merely an idol or a false god," but "the devil disguised as Almighty God—the antichrist."[25]

Apart from the ruling National Party, whose base remained primarily Afrikaner, only one other major group during the 1980s used ethnic identity to mobilize a following—the predominantly Zulu Inkatha movement led by Gatsha Buthelezi, a grandson of the last independent Zulu king. Although Inkatha leaders opposed apartheid, refusing to allow KwaZulu to become an "independent" homeland, they differed from the ANC on key strategic issues. In line with their procapitalist ideology, they opposed the efforts of antiapartheid activists to curtail foreign investment in South Africa. Through ethnic-based mobilization, they cultivated a popular following in rural KwaZulu/Natal and among Zulu migrant workers on the Rand. In the late 1980s and early 1990s, when the apartheid government increased support for Inkatha as a wedge against the UDF and the ANC, the ensuing bloody conflict between the two groups led to thousands of deaths.

By the mid-1980s, as antiapartheid organizing grew stronger, army and police crackdowns became more brutal. In July 1985, the night before the funeral of murdered eastern Cape activist Matthew Goniwe (which attracted an estimated 30,000 to 40,000 people from across the country), the government declared a state of emergency in selected areas, once again banning organizations and political meetings, and permitting the state to detain suspected activists indefinitely without charges or trial. Within eight months, nearly 8,000 people were imprisoned, and the ensuing violence had killed more than 250. Goniwe and the three other activists killed and mutilated by the security forces were known as the Cradock Four. Considering himself a revolutionary, Goniwe cautioned against drinking and sexual promiscuity: "If we are instruments of change," he said in a lecture to young people, "we MUST epitomize [the] society we want to bring about."[26]

Nearly a year later, anticipating mass protest on the tenth anniversary of the Soweto uprising, the state of emergency (which had briefly been lifted) was extended to the entire country and journalists were forbidden to issue reports of unrest. In this heated atmosphere, thousands of children were detained, leaving frantic families trying to obtain information about their arrest, imprisonment, and sometimes death at the hands of authorities. Funerals, the only large gatherings allowed, punctuated township life and turned into occasions for massive demonstrations and violent confrontation.

Funeral organized by the United Democratic Front (UDF) in 1985 for black activists killed by the police. With rising popular struggle in the mid-1980s, funerals became a key occasion for political speeches and popular mobilization. UWC-Robben Island Mayibuye Archives.

As military patrols and machine gun searches became daily events and many areas became virtually ungovernable, the tactics of the young "comrades" also grew more violent toward those they suspected of collaborating with authorities, their rough justice at times blurring the line between criminal and political behavior. In this chaotic atmosphere, even the widely revered Winnie Mandela was implicated when her bodyguards, known as the Mandela United Football Club, were charged with the beating death of fourteen-year-old activist Stompie Seipei in her home. Having suffered years of arrests, banning, banishment, and torture and venerated as the "mother of the nation," Mandela now became a controversial figure, even in the ANC and other antiapartheid groups.

With widespread television coverage of township violence, international outrage at events in South Africa escalated. Since the late 1970s the antiapartheid movement had urged major U.S. and European corporations to divest their holdings in the country. As an alternative, many American companies adopted a set of guidelines known as the Sullivan

In 1986, African vigilantes in alliance with the police destroyed the informal settlement of Crossroads near Cape Town. More than 60,000 people lost their homes. Although security forces were clearly involved, the government tried to distance itself from such attacks by describing them as "black on black" violence. UWC-Robben Island Mayibuye Archives.

Principles, named for the Rev. Leon Sullivan, the African American member of the General Motors board who proposed them. According to these guidelines, U.S. firms such as Ford, General Motors, and IBM with subsidiaries in South Africa pledged to end racial segregation in all workplace facilities and to promote equal employment practices for workers of all races. The Code of Conduct adopted by the European Economic Community also required companies to recognize black trade unions. Many universities and municipalities sold their holdings in firms that invested in South Africa and the exiled ANC began to mount an effective global campaign to free Nelson Mandela.

In the United States, these pressures combined with the ongoing international boycott of sporting events in which South African teams took part, the activities of longstanding anticolonial groups such as the American Committee on Africa, trade union campaigns, and the influence of new organizations, such as the Free South Africa Movement and TransAfrica (which staged widely publicized demonstrations at the South African Embassy), to put new pressure on the U.S. government. Amid all this publicity, in 1986 the U.S. Congress passed a bill that imposed sanctions against the apartheid regime, overriding the veto of President Ronald Reagan. Along with British Prime Minister Margaret Thatcher, Reagan continued to prefer a policy of "constructive engagement" with the white government. The legislation banned new investments and bank loans to South Africa, ended its air links with the United States, prohibited a range of South African imports from entering the country, and threatened to cut off aid to other countries that breached the arms embargo of South Africa—a measure that the United Nations had adopted in the early 1960s in the wake of the Sharpeville massacre. Under this pressure, many large companies such as General Motors, General Electric, IBM, and Coca Cola began closing down their South African subsidiaries, though other companies, and some black trade unions in South Africa, raised questions about whether withdrawal might ultimately be harmful to working-class Africans. Inkatha and the white liberal Progressive Federal Party, formed in 1977 as a merger between the Progressive Party and defectors from the United Party, voiced similar concerns about divestment.

In response to these fresh challenges, the apartheid government began to make cautious, but unexpected, moves in a new direction that built on the changes begun in the late 1970s, legalizing interracial marriage and recognizing a few integrated neighborhoods. More significantly, the hated pass laws were lifted in 1986, giving Africans the right to move freely without fear of arrest. Sensing the possibilities for change, key South

African business figures initiated informal discussions with leaders of the ANC in exile. A tentative proposal to release Mandela in exchange for an ANC truce was stopped cold, however, when Pretoria launched attacks on ANC bases in Zimbabwe, Botswana, and Zambia, where the ANC in exile had moved its headquarters. Perhaps most critically, and under conditions of absolute secrecy, government representatives began to meet with Nelson Mandela, who had been moved from Robben Island to Pollsmoor, a maximum security prison outside of Cape Town, and, in 1988, to his own cottage at Victor Verster prison in nearby Paarl, which he described as a "gilded cage." Confident that no one would recognize him, they occasionally took him out for a drive to give him the feel of the country after being locked away for so many years.

In 1989, two key events combined with these developments to catapult South Africa into a new era. With the collapse of the Soviet Union, the South African government lost its rhetorical rationale for opposing reforms—namely that it was holding the line against communism. More critical, in August 1989 the intransigent, hard-line P. W. Botha suffered a heart attack and F. W. de Klerk, the National Party leader, succeeded him as president. A pragmatist, de Klerk recognized that the government and the opposition movements had reached a stalemate. Within a few months he began to release key political prisoners, including Walter Sisulu and Govan Mbeki, and initiated plans to lift the bans on the ANC and the PAC and to free Mandela. With these moves, he hoped to open discussions about political change from a continued position of strength and power. What he envisioned at this point was not a transition to black majority rule, but a system of "power sharing" in a coalition government.

In the last section of his autobiography, written after his release from prison, Mandela reflected on his decision in 1985 to begin discussions with government officials. A surprise visit to him in the hospital from Kobie Coetsee, the minister of justice, followed by his return to a new cell in the Pollsmoor maximum security prison, led Mandela to a gradual realization. Now separated from the three colleagues with whom he had been moved from Robben Island in 1982, he wrote: "I . . . concluded that the time had come when the struggle could best be pushed forward through negotiations. If we did not start a dialogue soon, both sides would be plunged into a dark night of oppression, violence, and war. . . . It was clear to me that a military victory was a distant if not impossible dream. It simply did not make sense for both sides to lose thousands if not millions of lives in a conflict that was unnecessary. They must have known this as well. It was time to talk."[27]

Although both sides were now willing to negotiate, neither the process nor the outcome of these talks was predetermined. On February 11, 1990, the day the seventy-one-year-old Mandela was freed, an estimated half million people crowded along the forty-mile route between Paarl and Cape Town. With his wife Winnie at his side, a beaming Mandela was driven to the city center where he addressed the throngs of supporters who had waited hours to see him from the City Hall balcony. After paying tribute to those who had made "heroic sacrifices" in the cause of freedom, to supporters of the liberation struggle, and to his wife and family, he made it clear that the conflict with the apartheid regime had not ended. "We express the hope," he said, "that a climate conducive to a negotiated settlement will be created soon so that there may no longer be the need for the armed struggle." But, he added, "We have waited too long for our freedom. . . . Now is the time to intensify the struggle on all fronts. To relax our efforts now would be a mistake which generations to come will not be able to forgive. . . . It is only through disciplined mass action that our victory can be assured."[28]

CHAPTER 8

Democracy and Its Discontents

Mile-long lines stretched outside South Africa's polling stations in April 1994 as black and white voters waited patiently, often for more than six or seven hours, to cast ballots in the country's first democratic election. Eager with anticipation, Albertina Sisulu, voting at Orlando West in Soweto, told her daughter-in-law, "The excitement was unbelievable—going to jail, being forced to leave my children—it was all worth it to live to see this day."[1] One unemployed black man explained to a reporter, "Now I am a human being."[2]

Yet this outcome, democratic elections, did not come easily. In an interview soon after becoming the National Party leader in 1989, F. W. de Klerk fiercely opposed black majority rule, informing western diplomats, "Don't expect me to negotiate myself out of power."[3] As Mandela and the African National Congress (ANC) reentered the formal political arena, anger and suspicion seethed on both sides. Former exiles and guerrillas worried that once they returned, they would be seized and imprisoned; government officials feared that the ANC would take advantage of the amnesty to infiltrate guerrilla fighters into the country. As violence in the townships surged in the early 1990s, many members of MK hesitated to disband and give up their weapons as long as the government maintained heavily armed military and police forces. And although both sides recognized that the way forward lay in negotiations for a new constitution, strong divisions persisted.

Even after formal negotiations for a new democratic constitution began in December 1991, controversies continually endangered the deliberations. The first breakthrough had come early that year with Mandela's call for an all-party congress, which became known as CODESA (the Convention for a Democratic South Africa), to prepare an interim constitution. This document would provide for elections to a national assembly empowered to draft a permanent constitution. Early on, negotiators had agreed to the idea of a unified state with a multiparty democracy and guarantees of freedom and equality for all citizens. Yet groups jockeying for power under a new regime repeatedly threatened to disrupt the process. Inkatha and the representatives of Bophuthatswana held out for greater regional autonomy, the Pan Africanist Congress (PAC) and the Azanian People's Organization (AZAPO) opposed negotiations, and right-wing Afrikaners resisted ending white domination. In addition, women, absent from the initial negotiating team, succeeded in gaining representation only by forming a strong new organization, the National Women's Coalition, that united women of all races and political backgrounds. And, perhaps most critical, de Klerk and the National Party had translated their ideas of power sharing into plans for a bicameral legislature in which a Senate with regional, racial, and ethnic representation would balance a House of Representatives based on a universal franchise— thereby, in the words of a distinguished South African journalist, "giving the illusion of popular democracy but denying the substance."[4] The new executive would also represent this balance of interests.

Even as CODESA representatives began deliberating, popular discontent simmered on all sides of the political spectrum. Afrikaners opposed to any constitutional change charged de Klerk with acting without a mandate. To respond to conservative critics and solidify his base, de Klerk organized a whites-only referendum in March 1992 in which voters were asked whether the government should go forward with negotiations. With nearly 69 percent of voters opting to continue, he felt better able to disregard his extremist opponents.

Grassroots African constituencies, feeling marginalized in the deliberations, were incensed at the brutal violence that continued to terrorize township residents. Heavily armed men randomly attacked passengers on commuter trains and in the minivan taxis that ferried thousands of people daily between the townships and city centers. Although continuing to attribute such assaults to men from the Zulu-dominated migrant workers' hostels, more and more people began to believe that a government-backed "third force" was deliberately fomenting insecurity to weaken the ANC and forestall the negotiations. On June 17, 1992, thirty-eight people, mainly women and children, were slaughtered in their homes in Boipatong, a black community south of Johannesburg. Some observers identified the attackers as armed Zulu from a nearby hostel, while others reported seeing whites directing the violence. Two days later, when Mandela went to speak to crowds in a nearby community, angry residents condemned the ANC, charging that "You are like lambs while the government is killing us."[5]

Responding to the outrage at Boipatong, the ANC withdrew from the negotiations and issued a set of demands that would have to be met before talks could resume. When soldiers opened fire on 80,000 demonstrators in the Ciskei homeland two months later, Mandela compressed his fourteen initial demands into three, all geared toward stopping the violence: machetes (which Inkatha defended as "cultural weapons") must be banned, Inkatha-dominated hostels must be fenced in, and all disputed political prisoners must be released. More contentious, however, were unresolved issues about the distribution of power under a new government. At this point, a decisive breakthrough came from an unlikely source within the ANC—Communist Party militant and guerrilla leader Joe Slovo. Writing in the *African Communist* in August 1992, Slovo proposed a "sunset clause" that would accept compulsory power sharing for a fixed number of years and offer employment security to the predominantly white civil service to keep its employees from blocking movement toward democratic reform. Slovo based his argument on the assumption that Mandela and de Klerk had already accepted. Since the ANC was not dealing with a defeated enemy, compromise would be necessary in order to reach an agreement. In March 1993, the talks resumed.

On April 10, Janusz Walus, a violently anticommunist Polish immigrant with close ties to the right-wing Afrikaner Resistance Movement (AWB), assassinated the charismatic Communist Party leader Chris Hani in the driveway of his home in a racially mixed section of Boksburg, a predominantly white Johannesburg suburb. A neighbor reported that the killer approached Hani as he left his car, fired two shots into his chest, and then fired two more into his fallen body before fleeing from the scene. She memorized the license plate and called the police. Given his stature as a hero among young people who was widely discussed as a possible successor to Mandela as the country's president, the *New York Times* called his death a "staggering blow" to the ANC. The reporter observed that "Mr. Hani gave the congress credibility among its most disaffected constituents."[6]

Despite fears of a race war, however, the trauma seemed to strengthen the resolve of both sides to end the violence rather than to derail the talks once again. That evening, state television interrupted its programming so that Mandela could speak to the nation. Appealing to both blacks and whites, he explained: "A white man full of prejudice and hate came to our country and committed a deed so foul that our whole nation now teeters on the brink of disaster. But a white woman, of Afrikaner origin, risked her life so that we may know, and bring to justice, the assassin."[7]

From this point on, the negotiations survived violent efforts to disrupt the process from across the political spectrum, although Inkatha and the paramilitary AWB, dedicated to creating an Afrikaner state, continued to waver. Both agreed only at the last minute to take part in the elections, but not until after armed AWB members had staged an abortive attack within Bophuthatswana in support of Lucas Mangope's bid to retain power in this apartheid-created homeland. Buthelezi, still threatening to mount a guerrilla campaign against a new government, capitulated only when negotiators agreed to recognize the Zulu king and traditional authorities. In the end, despite their differences, the main parties acknowledged the truth of Mandela's blunt words to an Afrikaner group reminding them that a war to preserve their power was ultimately unwinnable and would reduce the country to ashes.

The final election results were a triumph for the ANC. The party won more than 62.6 percent of the vote and 252 seats in the new National Assembly, making Nelson Mandela the country's new president. The National Party (with 20.4 percent of the vote) and the Inkatha Freedom Party (with 10.5 percent of the vote) were the only other groups to attract substantial support. According to power-sharing guidelines agreed upon in the tortuous negotiations, National Party leader F. W. de Klerk became a deputy vice president. The distribution of the remaining seats among the conservative Afrikaner Freedom Front, the white liberal Democratic Party (formerly the Progressive Reform Party), the PAC, and the African Christian Democratic Party illustrates the wide range of political opinion. In a rarely noted, but no less dramatic transformation, 106 seats in the 400-member Parliament went to women, launching South Africa from 141st to seventh place in worldwide rankings of women in government. In a remarkable turnout, an estimated 90 percent of the population went to the polls.

Yet these elections marked only the beginning of a much longer journey to fulfill the dreams embodied in the remarkable new constitution adopted in 1996, which outlawed discrimination on grounds that include "race, gender, sex, pregnancy, marital status, ethnic or social origin, colour, sexual orientation, age, disability, religion, conscience, belief, culture, language, and birth" and established independent commissions to monitor human rights. These egalitarian ideals contrasted sharply with the material legacy of racial domination. In 1994, millions of people were jobless and homeless and millions more lacked running water, plumbing, or electricity. The per capita income of whites was nearly

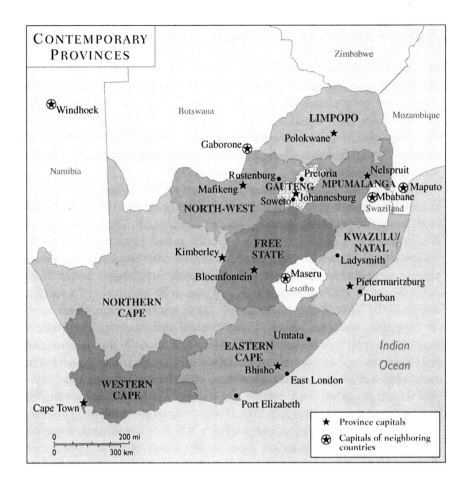

CONTEMPORARY
PROVINCES

Zimbabwe

Windhoek

Botswana

Mozambique

LIMPOPO

Gaborone

Polokwane

Namibia

Rustenburg
Mafikeng
NORTH-WEST

Pretoria
GAUTENG
Soweto
Johannesburg

Nelspruit
MPUMALANGA
Maputo
Mbabane
Swaziland

Kimberley

FREE
STATE

KWAZULU/
NATAL
Ladysmith

Bloemfontein

Maseru
Lesotho

Pietermaritzburg
Durban

NORTHERN
CAPE

Umtata

Indian

Ocean

EASTERN
CAPE
Bhisho

East London

WESTERN
CAPE

Port Elizabeth

Cape Town

0   200 mi
0   300 km

★   Province capitals

⊛   Capitals of neighboring
      countries

ten times that of the black majority. In a policy speech to Parliament
marking the end of his first hundred days in office, Mandela affirmed
his intention to speed the pace of change and reconciliation. "Millions
have suffered deprivation for decades and they have the right to seek
redress. They fought and voted for change; and change the people of
South Africa must have."[8]

The urgent need to narrow the gap between rich and poor made economic transformation a high priority of the ANC. Although in the early
1990s most of its leaders still believed in the socialist ideals of the Freedom Charter, the collapse of the Soviet Union prompted intense debates
about this facet of the party's ideology. Before coming to power, the
ANC had adopted the Reconstruction and Development Programme

(RDP) as a map for economic change. With a focus on reorganizing the economy to improve the lives of the poor, the RDP involved both the public and private sectors in building new homes, redistributing land, creating jobs, expanding health care and education, and increasing the number of people with running water, electricity, and modern sanitation facilities. The funds for these programs would come both from projected cuts in defense spending and from the anticipated "apartheid dividend"—an end to such expensive measures as maintaining multiple education departments.

Within two years, however, the effort to attract greater international investment prompted the new government to replace the RDP with a revised economic strategy known as Growth, Employment, and Redistribution (GEAR), a program better suited to the strict market-oriented guidelines of foreign donors from Western capitalist nations. A three-page government-sponsored advertising supplement to the *New York Times* in 2000 trumpeted this approach as promoting "a market economy by liberalizing commerce in favor of the private sector" and by "shedding the straitjacket of state control and throwing the window open to the private and foreign enterprise and investment." It promised that state-owned corporations launched by the apartheid government in transportation, telecommunications, arms manufacturing, and utilities would be offered for sale to the highest bidder. Racial inequality would be addressed through a "black economic empowerment" program, which encouraged foreign companies to work with local black entrepreneurs. Despite heavy criticism from trade unions and the Communist Party, which accused the ANC of abandoning its commitment to economic restructuring and redistribution of wealth, GEAR remained the program of Thabo Mbeki, who succeeded Mandela as president. The government's proposal for a basic income grant of R100 (then around $17.00)[9] per person per month regardless of income prompted Archbishop Desmond Tutu to argue, "We cannot glibly on full stomachs speak about handouts to those who often go to bed hungry."[10]

By 2007 efforts to improve life for the most impoverished communities had apparently met with some success. Since 1994 the government had built more than two million homes, about 85 percent of households had access to fresh water (up from 61 percent), more than 71 percent of homes had toilets connected to the sewage system (from 50 percent), and more than four million more homes had electric power—though at a quadrupled price many could not afford. Yet the income gap remained among the greatest in the world; more than 40 percent of South Africans lived on less than $1.15 a day and anger bubbled beneath the surface.

In May 2008 discontent turned into mob violence against immigrants from Mozambique, Zimbabwe, Malawi, and other African countries. Accusing foreigners of taking their jobs and housing, armed gangs began killing, beating, raping, and burning those identified as outsiders. By the end of the month at least fifty people had died and 35,000 were left homeless. One man interviewed in a township south of Johannesburg explained, "It is unfortunate that people got killed. But they had to go. They do not belong here taking our jobs."[11]

Land redistribution remained among the most pressing economic issues in rural areas. As South Africans closely watched the chaos and violence surrounding the popular seizures of white-owned farms in neighboring Zimbabwe, the Mandela and Mbeki governments tried to address the problem in a manner that did not alienate Afrikaner farmers by forcing them to vacate land they were unwilling to sell. Based on the meticulous records of land resettlement kept by the apartheid government, but also recognizing claims going back to 1913, the Land Claims courts were designed to restore land to those displaced by racially based expropriation. In one settlement, part of the Kruger National Park was returned to a community of 10,000 people who could then run their own game reserve. Despite such high profile cases, progress in redistributing land has been slow, leading government officials to consider ways to become more proactive in meeting the goal of transferring 30 percent of agricultural land to blacks by the end of 2014. In his State of the Nation address to Parliament in February 2008, President Mbeki promised a renewed commitment to land redistribution and restitution.

Along with seeking to right economic injustice, the country had to grapple with the legacy of violence. The Truth and Reconciliation Commission (TRC), charged with investigating flagrant human rights abuses committed under apartheid, began its work in 1996. With Archbishop Tutu as its chairperson, the TRC held hearings around the country at which victims were urged to testify about the atrocities they had witnessed and experienced, including murder, torture, and abduction. Under pressure from women activists, who realized that most of the initial testimonies by women related to abuses against men, three women-only hearings were held. In a supportive setting, women were encouraged to reveal their own experiences of rape and sexual abuse without fear or shame. In addition to the cathartic experience of sharing their stories, victims were promised millions of dollars in reparations. Between 1996 and 1998, 19,000 men, women, and children took the opportunity to provide evidence of systematic human rights violations.

In an effort to achieve both "truth" and "reconciliation," those who had committed murder and torture were offered the possibility of applying for amnesty in exchange for full confessions. Although some of their testimonies filled in the details of highly publicized cases, such as the gruesome death of Steve Biko at the hands of the police, officials at the highest level refused to cooperate with the commission. The final report censured the last two apartheid-era presidents, Botha and de Klerk, and accused the Inkatha Freedom Party of collaborating with the apartheid government in the slaughter of hundreds of people in the early 1990s. Under pressure not to absolve the liberation movement, the Commission also blamed the ANC for killing informers and for guerrilla raids that caused numerous civilian deaths. When the report was published, TRC chairman Archbishop Desmond Tutu argued bluntly: "I did not fight against people who thought they were God to replace them by others. Yesterday's oppressed could become tomorrow's oppressors."[12] In addition, the process raised critical questions about the relationship between reconciliation and justice, but prompted anger on the part of victims when the government failed to fully fund the reparations promised by the TRC.

Between 1994 and 2008, the political landscape remained relatively stable in South Africa, although the balance of power shifted decisively to the ANC. Mandela's deputy president Thabo Mbeki followed him as president in the elections of 1999 and 2004, when the party won 69.68 percent of the vote in a landslide victory. But despite the ANC's growing popularity, following in the footsteps of the widely revered and charismatic Mandela was not an easy task; initially Mbeki avoided kissing babies, dancing at public events, or talking directly to ordinary people. According to his biographer, "There was no way Mbeki was ever going to be adored the way Mandela was. So he advanced his career in a different way, by getting people to respect him, even if they did not like him."[13]

Mbeki's second term as president did not go smoothly, however. At a contentious ANC conference in December 2007, Mbeki lost his bid for continued party leadership to the more flamboyant and populist Jacob Zuma, whom Mbeki had dismissed as deputy president two years earlier in response to allegations of fraud and corruption. With presidents limited to two terms in office, Zuma's election placed him in line to assume the office in 2009. When in September 2008 a high court judge dismissed these charges on procedural grounds and ruled that Mbeki and his justice minister had colluded with prosecutors, the national executive committee of the ANC decided to "recall" Mbeki

Pedestrian walking past posters of Thabo Mbeki, the African National Congress candidate for president, before the April 2004 elections. AP Photo/Themba Hadebe.

from his post, forcing him to step down as president. Although the selection of Kgalema Motlanthe as interim president went smoothly, in early November a group of ANC members opposed to Zuma met to form a new breakaway political party, the Congress of the People.

The National Party declined precipitously with the demise of the apartheid regime. In 1996, feeling ignored when important decisions were made, de Klerk resigned his position as deputy president; seeking to shake off the pernicious legacy of apartheid, his party reconstituted itself as the New National Party. Nonetheless, it attracted only 7 percent of the voters in 1999. After receiving a mere 1.65 percent in 2004, the party decided to disband less than a year later. The Inkatha Freedom Party retained its core base in rural KwaZulu/Natal, but its support fell in each election. Only the liberal Democratic Alliance increased its share of the vote in 2004. Coming in a distant second, the party continued to attract English-speaking whites as well as wealthier Afrikaners, coloureds, and Indians by supporting free market economic policies, but has been unable to attract African voters.

Throughout their presidencies, Mandela and Mbeki sustained a commitment to interparty cooperation, gender equity, and nonracialism. Africans dominated party posts; but parliament was multiracial, members of all groups held ministerial positions, women were well represented, and Inkatha officials, including the party's head Gatsha Buthelezi, were included in the cabinet. While the ANC's economic policies strained its tripartite alliance with the South African Communist Party and COSATU (the still-powerful trade union federation), neither group withdrew support from the government.

In 1994, with a substantial number of women in parliament and a female speaker, Frene Ginwala, the legislature followed through on the government's commitment to improve women's lives, although insufficient resources and competing interests sometimes threatened to undermine these efforts. Mandela's government established "gender desks" in each ministry so that women's interests would be considered in all government programs, not relegated to areas of traditional concern such as family and social welfare, and new legislation was passed to protect victims of domestic violence; to change women's minority status under customary law; and to improve policies on maternity leave, sexual harassment, and workplace discrimination.

Despite the success of these efforts, violence against women has increased since 1994 and tensions embedded in the constitution—for example, between the abstract idea of human rights and the right to practice "traditional" cultures—posed a threat to gender equity, particularly in rural areas in which denying women the right to inheritance or to control over land could be justified as "tradition." A new law, the Communal Land Rights Bill, passed in 2004, made the situation worse by formally giving chiefs power over the land "and thus effectively," in the words of parliamentary gender activist Pregs Govender, "over the women who live on and work the land."[14] Mama Shabalala of the Rural Women's Movement echoed this critique and the political tensions over competing claims to empowerment: "If the Bill gives amakhosi (chiefs) power over land our suffering will become worse. We will go back to the old days—yet we have been looking forward to rights of our own."[15]

With the demise of apartheid, South Africa's pariah status in the international community vanished overnight. Building on Mandela's remarkable prestige, the new government moved quickly into a leadership position both in Africa and worldwide. In 1999, Mandela was called upon to mediate the violent ethnic conflict in Burundi; Mbeki helped to resolve crises in Congo, Rwanda, and Côte d'Ivoire, although critics, both internal and external, attacked him for not taking a stronger stand against flagrant abuses of government power in Zimbabwe. Moving to overcome its isolation from the rest of the continent, South Africa was instrumental in establishing the new African Union and in developing its socioeconomic program, NEPAD—the New Partnership for Africa's Development, and worked to strengthen SADC, the Southern African Development Community. Such initiatives, not always welcomed by other African countries, formed part of Thabo Mbeki's agenda in proclaiming an African Renaissance, in which South Africa intended to play a key role in revitalizing the continent by promoting democracy, new technology, and the philosophy of humanness, or *ubuntu*. Adding weight to this pan-African project, the government hosted major international conferences on sustainable development, racism, and HIV/AIDS—an event that drew critical attention to Thabo Mbeki's controversial stance on the causes and treatment of this devastating epidemic.

On January 6, 2005, looking frail but resolute, Nelson Mandela held a news conference surrounded by his grandchildren and his second wife, Graça Machel, to announce that his fifty-four-year-old son, Makgatho Mandela, had died of AIDS. Having campaigned tirelessly on behalf of people with this illness since he stepped down as president, Mandela announced that he was publicizing the cause of his son's death to help overcome the stigma that many South Africans continued to associate with the disease. He explained: "The only way to make it appear like a normal illness like TB, like cancer, is always to come out and say somebody has died because of HIV/AIDS, and people will stop regarding it as something extraordinary."[16]

With some 5.5 million HIV-positive people, the largest number in any single country, AIDS presented South Africa with a new and deadly challenge. Unlike the early stages of the disease in the United States, the majority of those infected were heterosexual, including a disproportionate number of young women. Acknowledging that he had not recognized the severity of the epidemic during his presidency, Mandela was among those who pushed the government to make antiretroviral drugs widely available in the country, not just to those who could afford private doctors. In 2002, Mandela publicly criticized President Thabo Mbeki and his health minister, who continued, despite biting local and international opposition, to question whether the HIV virus caused the illness and whether antiretroviral drugs helped to prolong life.

Among grassroots groups, the Treatment Action Campaign (TAC) was most visible in working to change government policy and popular attitudes. Its leader Zackie Achmat, a pioneering gay rights campaigner, turned his political acumen and the tactics of the antiapartheid struggle to the fight for free medication for those with AIDS. Achmat also waged a dramatic and risky personal battle, refusing antiretroviral therapy to combat his own infection until the government changed its stance. In addition to staging marches and civil disobedience, the group successfully sued the government over its initial refusal to provide medication to HIV-positive pregnant women to prevent the transmission of the virus to their children and pressured the international pharmaceutical industry into allowing South Africa (and other poor countries) access to low-cost antiretroviral drugs. In November 2003 the health minister announced a plan to distribute free medicine to millions infected with the virus and to establish a comprehensive program of AIDS education and prevention; critics charged the government with acting too slowly, however.

Although not without its difficulties, taking steps to create a unified national culture posed less of a challenge than fighting a devastating illness. In June 1995, only a year after historic elections brought the ANC to power, South Africa came to a standstill when the national rugby team played against New Zealand in the World Cup finals. Now that the international sports boycott had ended, the nation's teams could again compete on a world stage. When the South African team won, crowds gathered through the night to celebrate. As a historically white sport, with only one black player on the national team, rugby was not the obvious terrain for national reconciliation. Yet Mandela made the most of the opportunity, earning widespread admiration when he came out on the field wearing the team's bright green cap and shirt—the latter bearing the number of the white team captain.

This rugby match evoked a strong sense of national unity, but it also highlighted the impediments to creating and sustaining a new national culture to reflect South Africa's racial and ethnic diversity. In the months leading up to the election, the country had selected a boldly patterned new flag and merged *Nkosi Sikelel'iAfrika* and the Afrikaner *Die Stem* into a single national anthem. National holidays were soon adapted to new conditions. December 16, previously marking the slaughter of Zulu warriors at the Battle of Blood River, became the Day of Reconciliation; June 16, honoring the Soweto uprising, became Youth Day; and March 21, commemorating Sharpeville, became Human Rights Day. In an effort to move African culture to the center of national identity, the nine officially recognized African languages were slated to supplement English and Afrikaans for regular use in government communications.

Education, both in the schools and through public institutions such as museums and historical sites, was central to these transformations in social and cultural values. The effort to eliminate the vast resource gap between black and white schools and to strip away the legacy of Bantu education required wholesale administrative reorganization and consolidation—on the primary and secondary levels folding separate racial and ethnic systems into one, and in higher education creating a single racially integrated system. As the formerly white universities began to increase black enrollment, they turned to black scholars such as anthropologist, physician, and former Black Consciousness leader Mamphela Ramphele and novelist Njabulo Ndebele for new leadership. Alongside the schools and universities, new museums and national heritage sites mushroomed. Among the most prominent were the Apartheid Museum in Johannesburg and the District Six Museum in Cape Town. While helping to reconfigure the meaning of national identity, they also preserved the memory of the antiapartheid struggle for a young generation more attuned to *kwaito* music and their favorite soap operas than to staging mass demonstrations. The most popular of these sites, Robben Island, attracted 300,000 visitors a year, who made the boat trip from Cape Town to visit the cramped cells where Mandela, Sisulu, Sobukwe, and thousands of other political prisoners had been incarcerated.

All these efforts at national unity notwithstanding, racism remained a serious problem. Following the passage of a new antidiscrimination law in 2000, public hearings and a national conference revealed serious instances of racial abuse by employers and brutal attacks against Africans on white-owned farms. One farm worker spoke of an employer who routinely beat men, women, and children. "We never go to the police," he said, "it would just cause him [*sic*] to evict us."[17] Speaking at the conference, Mbeki appealed to whites to recognize the reality of racism and to join with blacks in creating a society in which "blackness will no longer be a belt of subservience."[18] These discussions also prompted black professionals to speak out about the more subtle insults they had experienced—as "second class appointees" who were promoted to high-level positions because of affirmative action, but not given work appropriate to their education or ability.

Cultural life in South Africa remained lively and inventive, as befits a small country with two winners of the Nobel Prize for literature, Nadine Gordimer and J. M. Coetzee. In novels such as *July's People*, *My Son's Story*, and *The House Gun*, Gordimer powerfully dramatized the injustices of apartheid and the pains of healing a divided society. Coetzee first attracted international acclaim with his darker, more abstract allegorical novel *Waiting for the Barbarians*, which posed profound moral and ethical questions about an imaginary empire responding to a perceived threat from nomadic barbarians. *Disgrace*, one of his more recent books, provoked controversy for its bleak and pessimistic portrayal of postapartheid life. Gordimer's and Coetzee's voices were heard among a widely acclaimed group of other writers such as Zakes Mda and Njabulo Ndebele, who also grappled with the moral and social dilemmas of apartheid and postapartheid life. Zulu poet Mazisi Kunene, who returned from thirty-four years of exile in 1993, was recognized as the first South African National Poet Laureate in 2005, fifteen months before his death. Alongside these literary voices, popular culture thrived in new musical forms such as *kwaito*, the popular dance music that emerged during the 1990s drawing in part on American hip-hop. Better known to international audiences, the male choral music of Ladysmith Black Mambazo led by Joseph Shabalala drew on Zulu music and dance as well as gospel and spirituals. On television, new soap operas became popular national sagas creating a middle-class fantasy world to which millions of viewers aspired. Also iconic of the new South Africa was the comic strip and television sitcom *Madam and Eve*, which portrayed the edgy relationship between a domestic worker and her liberal white employer with biting, gentle humor.

Reflecting a society that experienced an exhilarating breath of freedom, while grappling simultaneously with grinding poverty, soaring rates of unemployment and violent crime, the challenges of reconciliation, the scourge of AIDS, continuing white supremacist attitudes, and an unwelcome influx of impoverished immigrants from elsewhere on the continent, South Africa also confronted the tensions and contradictions involved in molding divergent traditions and value systems into a new national culture, and in becoming a society in which class divisions no longer fell so clearly along racial lines. While the constitution articulated a bold vision of liberal democratic citizenship and equality, many rural traditional leaders believed strongly in hereditary power and social hierarchy; while social conflicts animated lively debates in parliament, they also generated accusations of witchcraft and murders; while thousands of infected individuals struggled to obtain antiretroviral medication, many also sought cures from traditional healers, whom the government integrated into the official health care system; and despite a strong vein of social conservatism, in 2006 South Africa became the fifth country in the world and the first in Africa to legalize same-sex marriages.

Zakes Mda addresses this cultural gap in his novel, *The Heart of Redness*, published in 2000. Beginning with the split among the Xhosa over Nongqawuse's mid-nineteenth century prophecies of a future without European oppression, the story seamlessly blends historical and contemporary conflicts, paralleling the nineteenth-century division between "Believers" and "Unbelievers" with a current clash between supporters and opponents of a gambling casino and tourist resort. Throughout, the book integrates Xhosa words and concepts into English, and, by the end, merges the two plot lines into a single narrative. While focusing on one region and its longstanding clashes over culture, tradition, and modernity, Mda poses questions that were much more broadly applicable: of whether and how South Africa will be able to bridge the still stark divisions among its citizens, to fulfill the constitutional mandate of ensuring justice and equality for all, and to combine the nation's multiple voices into a single story.

Chronology

C. THIRD TO SEVENTH CENTURIES BCE
Farming and herding spread to southern Africa

1000–1300 CE
Settlements at Mapungwe and neighboring K2

1200–1500 CE
Settlement at Thulamela

1652
Dutch East India Company establishes refreshment station at the Cape of Good Hope

1688
French Huguenot refugees arrive

C. 1700
Tswana states emerge

1806
Britain recaptures Cape from Dutch

C. 1816
Shaka initiates the Zulu kingdom

1824
Moshoeshoe creates a new Sotho kingdom at Thaba Bosiu

1834
Slaves at Cape emancipated and then apprenticed for four years

1836–1840
Movement of Afrikaner settlers (Voortrekkers) into interior

1838
Battle of Blood River

1852 AND 1854
Britain recognizes Transvaal and the Orange Free State as independent Afrikaner republics

1856–1857
Xhosa "cattle killing"

1860
Indentured Indians brought to Natal

1867
Diamonds discovered in Griqualand West

1875
Accession of Khama in Tswana kingdom of Ngwato

1886
Gold discovered on the Witwatersrand

1894
Natal Indian Congress formed

1899–1902
South African War between the British and the Afrikaner republics

1910
Union of South Africa formed from the Cape Colony, Natal, the Orange Free State, and the Transvaal

1912
Launch of the South African Natives National Congress, which became the African National Congress (ANC)

1913
Natives Land Act passed
Women demonstrate against passes in the Orange Free State

1918
Afrikaner Broederbond formed

1919
Founding of the Industrial and Commercial Workers' Union (ICU)

1921
Formation of the Communist Party of South Africa (CPSA)

1922
Strike of thousands of white mine workers on the Witwatersrand

1930
White women win the right to vote

1936
Hertzog Bills abolish voting rights
for Cape Africans

1938
Centenary of the Great Trek celebrated

1943
Congress Youth League formed

1948
National Party elected to power under
banner of apartheid

1952
ANC and allied organizations
launch Defiance Campaign against
apartheid laws

1955
Freedom Charter adopted by the Congress
of the People

1956
Federation of South African Women leads
anti-pass demonstration in Pretoria

1959
Pan Africanist Congress (PAC) formed under
Robert Sobukwe

1960
March 21, Sharpeville massacre
Banning of ANC and PAC

1961
South Africa becomes a republic, leaving the
British Commonwealth

1963–1964
Trials of antiapartheid activists, including
sentencing of ANC leaders to life
imprisonment

1969
South African Students' Organization formed
with Steve Biko as leader

1976
June 16, Soweto students' uprising

1983
Formation of United Democratic Front to
oppose new tricameral parliament

1984–1986
Militant township resistance and violent
government crackdown

1985
South African Congress of Trade Unions
launched

1989
F. W. de Klerk became leader of the National
Party and then president

1990
Bans lifted on ANC, PAC, and South African
Communist Party (SACP) and Mandela
and other political prisoners released

1994
First democratic elections held with Nelson
Mandela elected president

1999 AND 2004
Thabo Mbeki elected and then reelected
president

Notes

CHAPTER 1

1. Mary D. Leakey, "Footprints in the Ashes of Time," *National Geographic* (April 1979), 453.

2. I. Schapera and E. Farrington, trans., *The Early Cape Hottentots* (1933; repr., Westport, CT: Negro Universities Press, 1933), 47.

3. Quoted in Monica Wilson, "The Hunters and Herders," in *A History of South Africa to 1870*, ed. Monica Wilson and Leonard Thompson (Boulder, CO: Westview Press, 1983), 61.

4. Nelson Mandela, *Long Walk to Freedom: The Autobiography of Nelson Mandela* (Boston: Little Brown and Co., 1994), 3.

5. Mandela, *Long Walk*, 8.

6. Mandela, *Long Walk*, 8.

7. Mandela, *Long Walk*, 10.

8. Mandela, *Long Walk*, 29.

9. Quoted in Monica Wilson, "The Nguni People," in Wilson and Thompson, *History of South Africa*, 82–83.

10. Harold Scheub, "And So I Grew Up: The Autobiography of Nongenile Masithathu Zenani," in *Life Histories of African Women*, ed. Patricia Romero (Atlantic Highlands, NJ: The Ashfield Press, 1988), 41.

11. Naboth Mokgatle, *The Autobiography of an Unknown South African* (Berkeley: University of California Press, 1971), 7.

12. Quoted in W. C. Willoughby, *The Soul of the Bantu* (Garden City, NY: Doubleday, Doran & Co., 1928), 94.

13. Scheub, "And So I Grew Up," 43–44.

14. Quoted in *Women Writing Africa: The Southern Region*, ed. M. J. Daymond, Dorothy Driver, Sheila Meintjes, Leloba Molema, Chiedza Musengezi, Margie Orford, and Nobantu Rasebotsa (New York: The Feminist Press, 2003), 86.

15. Liz Gunner and Mafika Gwala, trans. and ed., *Musho!: Zulu Popular Praises* (East Lansing: Michigan State University Press, 1991), 159.

16. Elizabeth Gunner, "Songs of Innocence and Experience: Women as Composers and Performers of *Izibongo*, Zulu Praise Poetry," *Research in African Literatures* 10 (1979), 246. The poem was recorded in Kwa/Zulu in 1975–1976.

CHAPTER 2

1. Kirstenbosch National Botanical Garden, official website, Van Riebeeck Hedge.

2. Quoted in I. Schapera and E. Farrington, trans., *The Early Cape Hottentots* (1933; repr., Westport, CT: Negro Universities Press, 1970), 45.

3. Schapera and Farrington, *Early Cape Hottentots*, 46.

4. Schapera and Farrington, *Early Cape Hottentots*, 47.

5. François Valentyn, quoted in Nigel Penn, *The Forgotten Frontier* (Athens: Ohio University Press, 2005), 43.

6. John Barrow, *Travels into the Interior of Southern Africa*, Parts 1 and 2 (London, 1804), 85, quoted in Penn, 122.

7. Robert Ross, *Cape of Torments: Slavery and Resistance in South Africa* (London: Routledge & Kegan Paul, 1983), 69.

8. Nigel Worden, *Slavery in Dutch South Africa* (Cambridge: Cambridge University Press, 1985), 64.

9. Barrow, *Travels*, 109.

10. Barrow, *Travels*, 110.

11. William J. Burchell, *Travels in the Interior of Southern Africa*, Vol. 1 (1822; repr., New York: Johnson Reprint Corp., 1968), 32–33.

12. Worden, *Slavery*, 103.

13. Burchell, *Travels in the Interior*, 70–71.

14. Richard Elphick and Robert Shell, "Intergroup Relations: Khoikhoi, Settlers, Slaves and Free Blacks, 1652–1795," in *The Shaping of South African Society, 1652–1840,* ed. Richard Elphick and Hermann Giliomee (Middletown, CT: Wesleyan University Press, 1988), 188.

15. Carl Peter Thunberg, *Travels at the Cape of Good Hope 1772–1775* (Cape Town: Van Riebeeck Society, 1986), 47–48.

CHAPTER 3

1. Robert Ross, *Cape of Torments: Slavery and Resistance in South Africa* (London: Routledge & Kegan Paul, 1983), 100.

2. Quoted in Ross, *Cape of Torments*, 143, n. 35.

3. John Philip, *Researches in South Africa: Illustrating the Civil, Moral, and Religious Condition of the Native Tribes*, 2 Vols. (1828; repr., New York: Negro Universities Press, 1969), 316.

4. Letter to the Editor, *De Zuid-Afrikaan*, 8 February 1839, quoted in John Edwin Mason, *Social Death and Resurrection: Slavery and Emancipation in South Africa* (Charlottesville: University of Virginia Press, 2003), 261.

5. I have retained the local spelling of "coloured" to indicate that this is a specifically South African category.

6. Quoted in Robert C.-H. Shell, "Between Christ and Mohammed: Conversion, Slavery, and Gender in the Urban Western Cape," in *Christianity in South Africa: A Political, Social, and Cultural History*, ed. Richard Elphick and Rodney Davenport (Berkeley: University of California Press, 1997), 276.

7. James Read, *The Kat River Settlement in 1851* (Cape Town: A. S. Robertson, 1852), 47, quoted in Robert Ross, *Status and Respectability in the Cape Colony, 1750–1870* (Cambridge: Cambridge University Press, 1999), 157.

8. Helen Bradford, "Not a Nongqawuse Story: An Anti-heroine in Historical Perspective," in *Women in South African History*, ed. Nomboniso Gasa (Cape Town: Human Sciences Research Council Press, 2007), quoting T. Pringle, "Letters from South Africa," *New Monthly Magazine* 19 (1827): 74. At this time the Dutch descendants called themselves Boers, meaning farmers.

9. Bradford, "Nongqawuse Story," 70.

10. J. B. Peires, *The House of Phalo: A History of the Xhosa People in the Days of Their Independence* (Berkeley: University of California Press, 1982), 91, quoting from Evidence of R. Aitchison, *Abo Com*, 9.

11. J. A. Millard, *Malihambe—Let the Word Spread* (Pretoria: Unisa Press, 1999); Dictionary of African Christian Biography website, quoting H. T. Cousins, *From Kaffir Kraal to Pulpit: The Story of Tiyo Soga* (London: S. W. Partridge, 1899), 146.

12. Peires, *House of Phalo*, 166, quoting from H. Smith-Grey, 7 January 1848, 51.

13. J. B. Peires, *The Dead Will Arise: Nongqawuse and the Great Xhosa Cattle-Killing Movement of 1856–7* (Bloomington: Indiana University Press, 1989), 79, quoting from W. W. Gqoba, "Siizatu Sokuxelwa Kwe Nkomo Ngo Nongqawuse," *Isigidimi SamaXosa*.

14. J. B. Peires, *Dead Will Arise*, xvi.

15. Nathaniel Isaacs, *Travels and Adventures in Eastern Africa*, Vol. 1 (Cape Town: The Van Riebeeck Society, 1836), 281.

16. Thomas Mofolo, *Chaka*, Daniel P. Kunene, trans. (London: Heinemann, 1981), 167.

17. Eugene Casalis, *My Life in Basuto Land* (London: Religious Tract Society, 1889), 176–77, quoted in Monica Wilson and Leonard Thompson, ed., *The Oxford History of South Africa to 1870* (New York: Oxford University Press, 1969), 401.

18. John A. Williams, *From the South African Past: Narratives, Documents, and Debates* (Boston: Houghton Mifflin, 1997), 77–78, citing G. W. Eybers, *Select Constitutional Documents Illustrating South African History* (London, 1918), 144–45.

CHAPTER 4

1. Robert I. Rotberg, with Miles F. Shore, *The Founder: Cecil Rhodes and the Pursuit of Power* (New York: Oxford University Press, 1988), 4.

2. *New York Times*, 25 July 1879.

3. Quoted in Paul Stuart Landau, *The Realm of the Word: Language, Gender, and Christianity in a Southern African Kingdom* (Portsmouth, NH: Heinemann, 1995), 27.

4. Psalms 68:31.

5. Brian Willan, ed., *Sol Plaatje: Selected Writings* (Athens: Ohio University Press, 1996), 64.

6. Quoted in Brian Willan, "An African in Kimberley: Sol T. Plaatje, 1894–1898," in *Industrialisation and Social Change in South Africa: African Class Formation, Culture, and Consciousness, 1870–1930*, ed. Shula Marks and Richard Rathbone (New York: Longman, 1982), 247.

7. From S. M. Molema, MS Biography of S.T. Plaatje, quoted in Brian Willan, "An African in Kimberley: Sol T. Plaatje, 1894–1898," in *Industrialisation and Social Change*, ed. Marks and Rathbone, 253.

8. "The Future of the Bill," Editorial in *Imvo Zabantsundu*, 15 August 1894, in *From Protest to Challenge: A Documentary History of African Politics in South Africa, 1882–1964*, ed. Thomas Karis and Gwendolen M. Carter, Vol. I: *Protest and Hope, 1882–1934*, ed. Sheridan Johns III (Stanford, CA: Hoover Institution Press, 1972), 17.

9. Bill Nasson, *The South African War, 1899–1902* (New York: Oxford University Press, 1999), 53.

10. Nasson, *South African War*, xiii.

11. Paul Kruger, *The Memoirs of Paul Kruger: Four Times President of the South African Republic* (Transvaal, 1902), 385.

12. Quoted in Peter Warwick, *Black People and the South African War 1899–1902* (Cambridge: Cambridge University Press, 1983), 112.

13. Quoted in James W. Muller, ed., *Churchill as Peacemaker* (New York: Cambridge University Press, 1997), 137, n. 97.

14. "Emily Hobhouse," www.anglo-boer.co.za/emily.html.

15. Warwick, *Black People*, 180.

16. *Milner Papers*, ii, 35–36, quoted in *The Oxford History of South Africa, II: South Africa 1870–1966*, ed. Monica Wilson and Leonard Thompson (Oxford: Clarendon Press, 1971), 330.

17. André Odendaal, *Black Protest Politics in South Africa to 1912* (Totowa, NJ: Barnes & Noble, 1984), 40.

CHAPTER 5

1. Reader's Digest, *Reader's Digest Illustrated History of South Africa* (Pleasantville, NY: Reader's Digest Association, 1988), 289.

2. *Illustrated History*, 266.

3. André Odendaal, *Black Protest Politics in South Africa to 1912* (Totowa, NJ: Barnes & Noble, 1984), 224.

4. Quoted in R. V. Selope Thema, "How Congress Began," *Drum* (July 1953).

5. Sol T. Plaatje, *Native Life in South Africa* (Athens: Ohio University Press, 1991), 21.

6. Quoted in Julia C. Wells, *We Now Demand! The History of Women's Resistance to Pass Laws in South Africa* (Johannesburg: Witwatersrand University Press, 1993), 21–22.

7. Quoted in Wells, *We Now Demand*, 42.

8. Quoted in Hermann Giliomee, "The Beginnings of Afrikaner Ethnic Consciousness," in *The Creation of Tribalism in Southern Africa*, ed. Leroy Vail (Berkeley: University of California Press, 1991), 49, n. 108.

9. Author's Interview, Johannesburg, July 1, 1983.

10. Carnegie Commission, *The Poor White Problem in South Africa*, Vol. 5 (Stellenbosch, South Africa: Pro Ecclesia, 1932), 198, quoted in Elsabe Brink, "Man-made Women: Gender, Class and the Ideology of the *Volksmoeder*," in *Women and Gender in Southern Africa to 1945*, ed. Cherryl Walker (London: James Currey, 1990), 282.

11. Quoted in Isabel Hofmeyr, "Building a Nation from Words: Afrikaans Language, Literature and Ethnic Identity, 1902–1924," in *The Politics of Race, Class & Nationalism in Twentieth Century South Africa*, ed. Shula Marks and Stanley Trapido (London: Longman, 1987), 110.

12. Quoted in Hofmeyr, "Building a Nation from Words," 113.

13. Leonard Thompson, *The Political Mythology of Apartheid* (New Haven, CT: Yale University Press, 1985), 40, citing *Die Groot Trek; Gedenkuitgawe van die Huisgenoot*, December 1938, 9.

14. Quoted in R. Hunt Davis Jr., "Charles T. Loram and an American Model for African Education in South Africa," *African Studies Review* 19(2) (September 1976): 93.

15. Quoted in Shula Marks, *The Ambiguities of Dependence in South Africa: Class, Nationalism, and the State in Twentieth-Century Natal* (Baltimore: Johns Hopkins University Press, 1986), 40.

16. Quoted in Marks, *Ambiguities*, 17.

17. Thomas Karis and Gwendolen Carter, ed., *From Protest to Challenge: A Documentary History of African Politics in South Africa*, Vol. 1: 1882–1934 (Stanford, CA: Hoover Institution Press, 1972), 215, quoting James S. Thaele in *The Workers' Herald*, 21 December 1923.

18. Charles van Onselen, *The Seed Is Mine: The Life of Kas Maine, A South African Sharecropper, 1894–1985* (New York: Hill & Wang, 1996), 151.

19. van Onselen, *Seed Is Mine*, 154.

20. Quoted in Helen Bradford, *A Taste of Freedom: The ICU in Rural South Africa, 1924–1930* (New Haven, CT: Yale University Press, 1987), 216.

21. Karis and Carter, eds., *From Protest*, Vol. I, 300.

22. *Report of the Commission of Inquiry into Secret Organizations*, 1965, 5, quoted in René de Villiers, "Afrikaner Nationalism," in *The Oxford History of South Africa*, Vol. II: *South Africa 1870–1996*, ed. Monica Wilson and Leonard Thompson (Oxford: Clarendon Press, 1971), 397.

23. Quoted in Hermann Giliomee, *The Afrikaners: Biography of a People* (Charlottesville: University of Virginia Press, 2003), 441.

24. Robert Edgar, *Because They Chose the Plan of God: The Story of the Bulhoek Massacre* (Johannesburg: Raven Press, 1995), 15.

25. *New York Times*, 18 November 1998.

26. Nelson Mandela, *Long Walk to Freedom: The Autobiography of Nelson Mandela* (Boston: Little Brown and Co., 1994), 44.

27. Modikwe Dikobe, *The Marabi Dance* (London: Heinemann, 1983), 1.

28. Peter Abrahams, *Tell Freedom: Memories of Africa* (New York: Alfred A. Knopf, 1966), 226.

29. "The All African Convention Proceedings and Resolutions of the AAC, December 15–18, 1935, in *From Protest to Challenge: A Documentary History of African Politics in South Africa, Vol. 2: 1935–1952*, ed. Thomas Karis and Gwendolen Carter (Stanford, CA: Hoover Institution Press, 1973), 31.

30. Quoted in Tom Lodge, *Black Politics in South Africa since 1945* (London: Longman, 1983), 8.

CHAPTER 6

1. Interview, www.anc.org.za/people/sisulu_a.html.

2. Elinor Sisulu, *Walter & Albertina Sisulu: In Our Lifetime* (Claremont, South Africa: David Philip, 2003), 88.

3. Sisulu, *Walter & Albertina*, 104.

4. Ray Phillips, "Social Work in South Africa," in *Christianity and the Natives of South Africa*, ed. and comp. Rev. J. Dexter Taylor (Lovedale, South Africa: Lovedale Institution Press, 1948), 150–51.

5. "To All Africans and Friends of Justice," Flyer issued by Dr. A. B. Xuma, March 21, 1947, in *From Protest to Challenge: A Documentary History of African Politics in South Africa, Vol. 2, 1935–1952*, ed. Thomas Karis and Gwendolen Carter (Stanford, CA: Hoover Institution Press, 1973), 273.

6. Karis and Carter, "Congress Youth League Manifesto," Issued by the Provisional Committee of the Congress Youth League, March 1944, in *Protest to Challenge, Vol. 2*, 306.

7. Karis and Carter, A. M. Lembede, "Policy of the Congress Youth League," *Inkundla ya Bantu*, May 1946, in *Protest to Challenge, Vol. 2*, 317.

8. Karis and Carter, Letter on the Youth League, from A. P. Mda to G. M. Pitje, 24 August 1948, in *Protest to Challenge, Vol. 2*, 320.

9. Quoted in Tom Lodge, *Black Politics in South Africa since 1945* (London: Longman, 1983), 22.

10. See "Statement by the National Party of South Africa," 29 March 1948, in Modern History Sourcebook, www.fordham.edu/halsall/mod/1948apartheid1.

11. *Reader's Digest Illustrated History of South Africa* (Pleasantville, NY: Reader's Digest Association, 1988), 379.

12. Nelson Mandela, *Long Walk to Freedom: The Autobiography of Nelson Mandela* (Boston: Little Brown and Co., 1994), 131.

13. Mandela, *Long Walk to Freedom*, 131.

14. Thomas Karis and Gail M. Gerhart, "Presidential Address by Chief A. J. Lutuli," in Thomas Karis and Gwendolen Carter, *From Protest to Challenge: A Documentary History of African Politics in South Africa, Vol. 3, 1953–1964* (Stanford, CA: Hoover Institution Press, 1977), 122, caps in original.

15. Karis and Carter, *Protest to Challenge, Vol. 3*, 122.

16. The Freedom Charter is reproduced in Karis and Carter, *Protest to Challenge, Vol. 3*, "Freedom Charter," adopted by the Congress of the People, 26 June 1955, 205.

17. Helen Joseph, *Side by Side: The Autobiography of Helen Joseph* (New York: William Morrow and Co., 1986), 63.

18. Lodge, *Black Politics*, 106, quoting Robert Resha, a militant ANC member, Sophiatown resident, and a key figure in the resistance campaign.

19. Cherryl Walker, *Women and Resistance in South Africa* (London: Onyx Press, 1982), 195.

20. Lodge, *Black Politics*, 151, from *Bantu World*, 8 October 1955.

21. Lodge, *Black Politics*, 83, from *Golden City Post*, 29 March 1959.

22. Edward Roux, *Time Longer Than Rope* (Madison: University of Wisconsin Press, 1964), 407.

23. Quoted in Robert Kinloch Massie, *Loosing the Bonds: The United States and South Africa in the Apartheid Years* (New York: Doubleday, 1997), 66.

24. Quoted in Lodge, *Black Politics*, 243, from the *Rand Daily Mail*, 23 March 1963.

25. Nelson Mandela, *No Easy Walk to Freedom* (1965; repr., London: Heinemann, 1989), 189.

CHAPTER 7

1. Quoted in Robert Kinloch Massie, *Loosing the Bonds: The United States and South Africa in the Apartheid Years* (New York: Doubleday, 1997), 70.

2. *This Is South Africa* (Pretoria: Bureau for Information, 1988), 23.

3. Helen Suzman, *In No Uncertain Terms: A South African Memoir* (New York: Alfred A. Knopf, 1993), 70.

4. Suzman, *No Uncertain Terms*, 96.

5. Quoted in Ntongela Masilela, "Mazisi Kunene (1930–2006): An Appreciation," August 13, 2006, www.cas.org.za/projects/masilela.doc.

6. Joseph Lelyveld, *Move Your Shadow: South Africa, Black and White* (New York: Times Books, 1985), 123.

7. Lelyveld, *Move Your Shadow*, 123–24.

8. Lelyveld, *Move Your Shadow*, 125.

9. Quoted in Bengt G. M. Sundkler, *Bantu Prophets in South Africa* (1948; repr., London: Oxford University Press), 304.

10. Sundkler, *Bantu Prophets*, 336.

11. Lewis DeSoto, *A Blade of Grass* (New York: HarperCollins, 2003), "About the Author," 4.

12. Rian Malan, *My Traitor's Heart* (London: Vintage, 1990), 41.

13. Quoted in Hermann Giliomee, *The Afrikaners: Biography of a People* (Charlottesville: University of Virginia Press, 2003), 554.

14. Giliomee, *The Afrikaners*, 556.

15. Nelson Mandela, *Long Walk to Freedom: The Autobiography of Nelson Mandela* (Boston: Little Brown and Co., 1994), 341.

16. Steve Biko, *I Write What I Like: Selected Writings* (London: Bowerdean Press, 1978), 92.

17. Quoted in Steven Friedman, *Building Tomorrow Today: African Workers in Trade Unions 1910–1984* (Johannesburg: Ravan Press, 1987), 46.

18. Mark Mathabane, *Kaffir Boy: The True Story of a Black Youth's Coming of Age in Apartheid South Africa* (New York: New American Library, 1986), 259 and Winnie Mandela, *Part of My Soul Went With Him*, ed. Anne Benjamin and adapted by Mary Benson (New York: Norton, 1984), 112.

19. Mathabane, *Kaffir Boy*, 259.

20. Steve Biko, "Our Strategy for Liberation," in Biko, *I Write What I Like*, 145–46.

21. *Time*, 12 December 1977.

22. Massie, *Loosing the Bonds*, 423.

23. From "The Role of Women in the Struggle for Liberation in Zimbabwe, Namibia & South Africa," paper presented at the UN Conference on Women, Copenhagen, 14–30 July 1980, quoted in Hilda Bernstein, *For Their Triumphs and for Their Tears: Women in Apartheid South Africa* (London: International Defence and Aid Fund for Southern Africa, 1985), 43.

24. These figures are cited in Bernstein, *For Their Triumphs*, 45. It is important to note that these official statistics do not include marriages according to African ceremonies, still extremely prevalent in rural areas.

25. From *The Kairos Document: Challenge to the Church: A Theological Comment on the Political Crisis in South Africa* (Johannesburg: 1986), 7, quoted in Allister Sparks, *The Mind of South Africa* (New York: Alfred A. Knopf, 1990), 287.

26. Quoted in Steven Mufson, *Fighting Years: Black Resistance and the Struggle for a New South Africa* (Boston: Beacon Press, 1990), 112.

27. Mandela, *Long Walk*, 525.

28. "Nelson Mandela's Address to Rally in Cape Town on His Release from Prison," February 11, 1990, www.anc.org.za/ancdocs/history/mandela/1990/release.

CHAPTER 8

1. Quoted in Elinor Sisulu, *Walter & Albertina Sisulu: In Our Lifetime* (Claremont, South Africa: David Philip, 2003), 621.

2. Allister Sparks, *Tomorrow Is Another Country: The Inside Story of South Africa's Road to Change* (Chicago: University of Chicago Press, 1996), 227.

3. Allister Sparks, *The Mind of South Africa* (New York: Alfred A. Knopf, 1990), 370.

4. Sparks, *Tomorrow Is Another Country,* 127.

5. Sparks, *Tomorrow Is Another Country*, 146.

6. Bill Keller, *New York Times*, April 11, 1993.

7. Sparks, *Tomorrow Is Another Country*, 189.

8. Bernard Makhosezwe Magubane, "Reflections on the Challenges Confronting Post-Apartheid South Africa," Management of Social Transformations, Discussion Paper Series No. 7, www.unesco.org/shs/most.

9. Fluctuations of both currencies make it impossible to give an exact equivalent figure.

10. *Mail & Guardian*, 23 November 2004.

11. *Guardian*, 20 May 2008.

12. Quoted in *The Independent*, 31 October 1998.

13. "The Guardian Profile: Thabo Mbeki," 8 April 2004, quoting Mark Gevisser.

14. Pregs Govender, "Reasserting Politics as the Power of Love and Courage," 8, soc.kuleuven.be/pol/lpra/docs/cal_govender.

15. Quoted in Govender, "Reasserting Politics," 8.

16. *New York Times*, 7 January 2005.

17. Reported in *Unequal Protection: The State Response to Violent Crime on South African Farms* (New York: Human Rights Watch, 2001) (online).

18. BBC News, 30 August 2000.

Further Reading

GENERAL

Beinart, William. *Twentieth-Century South Africa*, 2nd ed. Oxford: Oxford University Press, 2001.

Davenport, Rodney, and Christopher Saunders. *South Africa: A Modern History*, 5th ed. New York: St. Martin's, 2000.

MacKinnon, Aran S. *The Making of South Africa: Culture and Politics*. Upper Saddle River, NJ: Pearson Prentice Hall, 2004.

Reader's Digest. *Reader's Digest Illustrated History of South Africa: The Real Story*. Pleasantville, NY: Reader's Digest, 1995.

Ross, Robert. *A Concise History of South Africa*. Cambridge: Cambridge University Press, 1999.

Thompson, Leonard. *A History of South Africa*, 3rd ed. New Haven: Yale University Press, 2000.

Williams, John A. *From the South African Past: Narratives, Documents, and Debates*. Boston: Houghton Mifflin, 1997.

Worden, Nigel. *The Making of Modern South Africa: Conquest, Segregation and Apartheid*. Malden, MA: Blackwell, 2000.

EARLY HISTORY

Boonzaier, Emile, Candy Malherbe, Andy Smith, and Penny Berens. *The Cape Herders: A History of the Khoikhoi of Southern Africa*. Athens: Ohio University Press, 1996.

Deacon, H. J., and Janette Deacon. *Human Beginnings in South Africa: Uncovering the Secrets of the Stone Age*. Walnut Creek, CA: AltaMira Press, 1999.

Hall, Martin. *Farmers, Kings, and Traders: The People of Southern Africa, 200–1860*. Chicago: University of Chicago Press, 1990.

Smith, Andy, Candy Malherbe, Mat Guenther, and Penny Berens. *The Bushmen of Southern Africa: A Foraging Society in Transition*. Athens: Ohio University Press, 2000.

SOCIAL HISTORY

Atkins, Keletso. *The Moon Is Dead! Give Us Our Money! The Cultural Origins of an African Work Ethic, Natal, South Africa, 1843–1900*. Portsmouth, NH: Heinemann, 1993.

Beinart, William. *The Rise of Conservation in South Africa: Settlers, Livestock and the Environment, 1770–1950*. New York: Oxford University Press, 2003.

Beinart, William, and Colin Bundy. *Hidden Struggles in Rural South Africa: Politics & Popular Movements in the Transkei and Eastern Cape, 1890–1930*. Berkeley: University of California Press, 1987.

Bundy, Colin. *The Rise & Fall of the South African Peasantry*. Berkeley: University of California Press, 1979.

Crais, Clifton C. *White Supremacy and Black Resistance in Pre-Industrial South Africa: The Making of the Colonial Order in the Eastern Cape, 1770–1865*. Cambridge: Cambridge University Press, 1992.

Eldredge, Elizabeth A. *A South African Kingdom: The Pursuit of Security in Nineteenth-Century Lesotho*. Cambridge: Cambridge University Press, 1993.

Elphick, Richard. *Khoikhoi and the Founding of White South Africa*. New Haven: Yale University Press, 1985.

Ethrington, Norman. *The Great Treks: The Transformation of Southern Africa, 1815–1854*. Harlow, England: Longman, 2001.

Fredrickson, George M. *White Supremacy: A Comparative Study in American and South African History*. New York: Oxford University Press, 1981.

Giliomee, Hermann. *The Afrikaners: Biography of a People*. Charlottesville: University of Virginia Press, 2003.

Guy, Jeff. *The Destruction of the Zulu Kingdom*. London: Longman, 1979.

Marks, Shula. *Reluctant Rebellion: The 1906–08 Disturbances in Natal*. Oxford: Clarendon Press, 1970.

Mason, John Edwin. *Social Death and Resurrection: Slavery and Emancipation in South Africa*. Charlottesville: University of Virginia Press, 2003.

Nasson, Bill. *The South African War 1899–1902*. New York: Oxford University Press, 1999.

Odendaal, André. *Black Protest Politics in South Africa to 1912*. Totowa, NJ: Barnes & Noble Books, 1984.

Omer-Cooper, J. D. *The Zulu Aftermath: A Nineteenth Century Revolution in Bantu Africa*. Evanston, IL: Northwestern University Press, 1966.

Peires, J. B. *The House of Phalo: A History of the Xhosa People in the Days of their Independence*. Berkeley: University of California Press, 1982.

———. *The Dead Will Arise: Nongqawuse and the Great Xhosa Cattle-Killing Movement of 1856–7*. Bloomington: Indiana University Press, 1989.

Penn, Nigel. *The Forgotten Frontier: Colonist and Khoisan on the Cape's Northern Frontier in the 18th Century*. Athens: Ohio University Press, 2005.

Ross, Robert. *Status and Respectability in the Cape Colony, 1750–1870: A Tragedy of Manners*. Cambridge: Cambridge University Press, 1999.

Turrell, Robert Vicat. *Capital and Labour on the Kimberley Diamond Fields, 1871–1890*. Cambridge: Cambridge University Press, 1987.

Van Onselen, Charles. *Studies in the Social and Economic History of the Witwatersrand, 1886–1914*. Vol. 1: *New Babylon*. Vol. 2: *New Nineveh*. New York: Longman, 1982.

Warwick, Peter. *Black People and the South African War, 1899–1902*. Cambridge: Cambridge University Press, 1983.

Worden, Nigel. *Slavery in Dutch South Africa*. Cambridge: Cambridge University Press, 1985.

Worger, William H. *South Africa's City of Diamonds: Mine Workers and Monopoly Capitalism in Kimberley, 1867–1895*. New Haven: Yale University Press, 1987.

SEGREGATION AND APARTHEID

Beinart, William, and Saul Dubow, eds. *Segregation and Apartheid in Twentieth-Century South Africa*. London: Routledge, 1995.

Biko, Steve. *I Write What I Like*. San Francisco: Harper & Row, 1986.

Bradford, Helen. *A Taste of Freedom: The ICU in Rural South Africa, 1924–1930*. New Haven: Yale University Press, 1987.

Buntman, Fran Lisa. *Robben Island and Prisoner Resistance to Apartheid*. New York: Cambridge University Press, 2003.

Campbell, James T. *Songs of Zion: The African Methodist Church in the United States and South Africa*. New York: Oxford University Press, 1995.

Cell, John W. *The Highest Stage of White Supremacy: The Origins of Segregation in South Africa and the American South*. New York: Cambridge University Press, 1987.

Clark, Nancy L., and William H. Worger. *South Africa: The Rise and Fall of Apartheid*. New York: Longman, 2004.

Coplan, David B. *In Township Tonight! South Africa's Black City Music and Theatre*. London: Longman, 1985.

Dubow, Saul. *Racial Segregation and the Origins of Apartheid in South Africa, 1919–36*. Oxford: Macmillan, 1989.

Fredrickson, George M. *Black Liberation: A Comparative History of Black Ideologies in the United States and South Africa*. New York: Oxford University Press, 1995.

Halisi, C. R. D. *Black Political Thought in the Making of South African Democracy*. Bloomington: Indiana University Press, 1999.

Krikler, Jeremy. *White Rising: The 1922 Insurrection and Racial Killing in South Africa*. Manchester: Manchester University Press, 2005.

Lelyveld, Joseph. *Move Your Shadow: South Africa, Black and White*. New York: Times Books, 1985.

Lodge, Tom. *Black Politics in South Africa since 1945*. London: Longman, 1983.

Magubane, Bernard. *South Africa: From Soweto to Uitenhage*. New York: Monthly Review Press, 1989.

Mandela, Nelson. *No Easy Walk to Freedom*. London: Heinemann, 1989.

Marks, Shula, and Stanley Trapido, eds. *The Politics of Race, Class & Nationalism in Twentieth Century South Africa*. London: Longman, 1987.

Massie, Robert Kinloch. *Loosing the Bonds: The United States and South Africa in the Apartheid Years*. New York: Doubleday, 1997.

Minter, William, Gail Hovey, and Charles Cobb Jr., eds. *No Easy Victories: African Liberation and American Activists over a Half Century, 1950–2000*. Trenton, NJ: Africa World Press, 2008.

Mkhondo, Rich. *Reporting South Africa*. Portsmouth, NH: Heinemann, 1993.

Moody, T. Dunbar. *The Rise of Afrikanerdom: Power, Apartheid, and the Afrikaner Civil Religion*. Berkeley: University of California Press, 1975.

Nesbitt, Francis Njubi. *Race for Sanctions: African Americans Against Apartheid, 1946–1994*. Bloomington: Indiana University Press, 2004.

Plaatje, Solomon. *Native Life in South Africa*. New York: Negro Universities Press, 1969.

Posel, Deborah. *The Making of Apartheid, 1948–1961*. New York: Oxford University Press, 1997.

Sparks, Allister. *The Mind of South Africa*. New York: Knopf, 1990.

Sundkler, Bengt G. M. *Bantu Prophets in South Africa*. London: Oxford University Press, 1961.

Walshe, Peter. *The Rise of African Nationalism in South Africa: The African National Congress, 1912–1952*. Berkeley: University of California Press, 1971.

BIOGRAPHIES AND AUTOBIOGRAPHIES

Abrahams, Peter. *Tell Freedom: Memories of Africa*. New York: Knopf, 1966.

Callinicos, Luli. *Oliver Tambo: Beyond the Engeli Mountains*. Claremont, South Africa: 2004.

Edgar, Robert R., and Hilary Sapire. *African Apocalypse: The Story of Nontetha Nkwenkwe, a Twentieth-Century Prophet*. Athens: Ohio University Center of International Studies, 2000.

First, Ruth and Ann Scott. *Olive Schreiner: A Biography*. New York: Schocken Books, 1980.

Gish, Steven. *Alfred B. Xuma: African, American, South African*. New York: New York University Press, 2000.

Gumede, William Mervin. *Thabo Mbeki and the Battle for the Soul of the ANC*. Cape Town: Struik, 2005.

Higgs, Catherine. *The Ghost of Equality: The Public Lives of D.D.T. Jabavu of South Africa, 1885–1959*. Athens: Ohio University Press, 1997.

Joseph, Helen. *Side By Side: The Autobiography of Helen Joseph*. New York: Morrow, 1986.

Kuzwayo, Ellen. *Call Me Woman*. San Francisco: Spinster's Ink, 1985.

Lodge, Tom. *Mandela: A Critical Life*. New York: Oxford University Press, 2006.

Mandela, Nelson. *Long Walk to Freedom: The Autobiography of Nelson Mandela*. Boston: Little Brown, 1995.

Mathabane, Mark. *Kaffir Boy: The True Story of a Black Youth's Coming of Age in Apartheid South Africa*. 1986; repr. New York: Plume, 1990.

McCord, Margaret. *The Calling of Katie Makanya*. New York: Wiley, 1995.

Mphahlele, Es'kia. *Down Second Avenue*. Boston: Faber and Faber, 1985.

Ramphele, Mamphela. *Across Boundaries: The Journey of a South African Woman Leader*. New York: Feminist Press, 1996.

Sisulu, Elinor. *Walter & Albertina Sisulu: In Our Lifetime*. London: Abacus (Little Brown Book Group), 2003.

Van Onselen, Charles. *The Seed Is Mine: The Life of Kas Maine, a South African Sharecropper, 1894–1985*. New York: Hill and Wang, 1996.

Willan, Brian. *Sol Plaatje: South African Nationalist, 1876–1932*. Berkeley: University of California Press, 1984.

Woods, Donald. *Biko*. New York: Penguin, 1979.

WOMEN, GENDER, AND FAMILY

Berger, Iris. *Threads of Solidarity: Women in South African Industry, 1900–1980*. Bloomington: Indiana University Press, 1992.

Bernstein, Hilda. *For Their Triumphs and for Their Tears: Women in Apartheid South Africa*. London: International Defence and Aid for Southern Africa, 1985.

Bozzoli, Belinda, with the assistance of Mmantho Nkotsoe. *Women of Phokeng: Consciousness, Life Strategy, and Migrancy in South Africa, 1900–1983*. Portsmouth, NH: Heinemann, 1991.

Daymond, M. J., Dorothy Driver, Sheila Meintjes, Leloba Molema, Chiedza Musengezi, Margie Orford, and Nobantu Rasebotsa, eds. *Women Writing Africa: The Southern Region*. New York: Feminist Press, 2003.

Hassim, Shireen. *Women's Organizations and Democracy in South Africa: Contesting Authority*. Madison: University of Wisconsin Press, 2005.

Marks, Shula, ed. *Not Either an Experimental Doll: The Separate Worlds of Three South African Women*. Bloomington: Indiana University Press, 1988.

Morrell, Robert, ed. *Changing Men in Southern Africa*. London: Zed Books, 2001.

Walker, Cherryl, ed. *Women and Gender in Southern Africa to 1945*. London: James Currey, 1990.

———. *Women and Resistance in South Africa*. New York: Monthly Review Press, 1991.

Wells, Julia C. *We Now Demand! The History of Women's Resistance to Pass Laws in South Africa*. Johannesburg: Witwatersrand University Press, 1993.

FICTION

Coetzee, J. M. *Waiting for the Barbarians*. New York: Penguin, 1982.

Dikobe, Modikwe. *The Marabi Dance*. London: Heinemann, 1983.

Gordimer, Nadine. *July's People*. New York: Penguin, 1982.

Kunene, Mazisi. *Emperor Shaka the Great*. London: Heinemann, 1979.

Mda, Zakes. *The Heart of Redness*. New York: Farrar, Strauss & Giroux, 2000.

Mofolo, Thomas. *Chaka*. London: Heinemann, 1981.

Mzamane, Mbulelo Vizkhungo. *The Children of Soweto*. Burnt Mill, England: Longman, 1982.

Ndebele, Njabulo S. *The Cry of Winnie Mandela*. Cape Town: David Philip, 1983.

Plaatje, Sol T. *Mhudi*. Washington, DC: Three Continents Press, 1978.

Schreiner, Olive. *The Story of an African Farm*. Oxford: Oxford University Press, 1998.

POSTAPARTHEID SOUTH AFRICA

Asmal, Kader, Louise Asmal, and Ronald Suresh Roberts. *Reconciliation Through Truth: A Reckoning of Apartheid's Criminal Governance*. New York: St. Martin's, 1997.

Graybill, Lyn S. *Truth & Reconciliation in South Africa: Miracle or Model?* Boulder, CO: Lynne Rienner, 2002.

Krog, Antjie. *Country of My Skull: Guilt, Sorrow, and the Limits of Forgiveness in the New South Africa*. New York: Three Rivers Press, 2000.

Lodge, Tom. *Politics in South Africa: From Mandela to Mbeki*. Bloomington: Indiana University Press, 2002.

Nuttall, Sarah, and Cheryl-Ann Michael, eds. *Senses of Culture: South African Culture Studies*. New York: Oxford University Press, 2000.

Sparks, Allister. *Beyond the Miracle: Inside the New South Africa*. Chicago: University of Chicago Press, 2003.

Web Sites

African National Congress
www.anc.org
ANC news and updates, including full-text historical documents and links to affiliated organizations.

Africa South of the Sahara: Selected Internet Resources
www-sul.stanford.edu/depts./ssrg/Africa
A comprehensive Internet site from the Stanford University Library Africa Collection. The South Africa page includes links to thirty-three topical listings, each with a comprehensive list of links to relevant websites. An outstanding comprehensive resource.

Aluka
www.aluka.org
Online digital library with extensive material on struggles for freedom in southern Africa, including journal articles, reports, correspondence, and interviews.

Congress of South African Trade Unions
www.cosatu.org.za
Information and links relating to the trade union federation that is now part of the government's tripartite alliance with the ANC and the SACP.

Digital Imaging Project of South Africa (DISA)
disa.nu.ac.za
Thirty-nine periodicals on the growth of opposition to apartheid, 1960–1990, being digitized for free online access.

District Six Museum
www.districtsix.co/za
Documents the forced removals in Cape Town and reconstructs the history of the community.

H-South Africa
H-SAfrica@h-net.msu.edu
Electronic postings and discussion on all aspects of South African history.

Iziko—Museums of Cape Town
www.museums.org.za/iziko
Amalgamation of five formerly independent museums and galleries, including exhibits on many aspects of South African history.

Mail & Guardian Online and Mail & Guardian Archives
www.mg.co/za
Daily online version of South African weekly newspaper.

Overcoming Apartheid, Building Democracy
www.overcomingapartheid.msu.edu
Stories of lives and actions of proponents of democracy both during and after the apartheid years.

Robben Island Museum
www.robben-island.org.za
Museum documenting South Africa's liberation struggles and the island's political and universal symbolism.

South African Communist Party
www.sacp.org.za
Information and links relating to this member of the government's tripartite alliance with the ANC and COSATU.

South African Government Online
www.gov.sa
Current and archived government information, including speeches, documents, biographies, departments, and issues.

South African History Archive
www.wits.ac.za/saha
Archive documenting struggles for justice in South Africa. Includes research links on a range of contemporary issues.

South African History Online
www.sahistory.org.za
Site concerned with critically reexamining South African history and strengthening history teaching. Topical links include online library and archive.

UNESCO World Heritage: South Africa
whc.unesco.org/en/statesparties/za
Information on the World Heritage sites located in South Africa.

Acknowledgments

A number of people contributed to this book's research and writing. First, I would like to thank Noelle Colquhoun Sullivan for her prodigious research assistance on the first two chapters. I only regret that she went on to study for her doctorate in anthropology long before the book was completed. Discussions of African history with current graduate students David Jones, Michael Panzer, and Shoshana Stein and former students Jessica Powers, Jennifer Hays, and Wendy Urban-Meade have stimulated my thinking on many issues.

Those who have read and commented on the manuscript deserve particular thanks. Nancy Toff, my editor at Oxford University Press, has been a pleasure to work with. Her exacting, but always supportive, suggestions have enhanced the book, in part by sending me back to primary sources for illuminating historical insights. Similarly, the series editors, Bonnie Smith and Anand Yang, each offered distinctive and valuable comments on the original draft. Their respective expertise in European and Asian history in a global context has improved the book substantially. I am also grateful to two anonymous readers whose detailed suggestions prompted me to rethink some sections of the book and to add new material to others, and to the third reader, Shula Marks. As a longtime friend and colleague, her immense knowledge has deepened my understanding of South African history. Her willingness to read the manuscript and the care she took in doing so are warmly appreciated. Finally, Ron Berger read the manuscript with astonishing thoughtfulness and insight. His unerring instincts and suggestions as both a writer and a historian, along with his love and encouragement, have enriched the book in immeasurable ways.

Index

The New Oxford World History

General Editors

BONNIE G. SMITH
Rutgers University

ANAND A. YANG
University of Washington

Editorial Board

DONNA GUY
Ohio State University

KAREN ORDAHL KUPPERMAN
New York University

MARGARET STROBEL
University of Illinois, Chicago

JOHN O. VOLL
Georgetown University

The New Oxford World History
provides a comprehensive, synthetic
treatment of the "new world history"
from chronological, thematic, and
geographical perspectives, allowing
readers to access the world's complex
history from a variety of conceptual,
narrative, and analytical viewpoints as
it fits their interests.

Iris Berger is professor of history,
Africana studies, and women's studies
at the University at Albany–State
University of New York. She earned her
M.A. in African History and her Ph.D
in African History and Comparative
Third-World History at the University
of Wisconsin at Madison. She was
president of the African Studies
Association in 1995–96. Her books on
African history include *Threads of
Solidarity: Women in South African
Industry, 1900–1980*, *Women in Sub-
Saharan Africa*, with E. Frances White,
Women and Class in Africa, edited
with Claire Robertson, and the award-
winning *Religion and Resistance: East
African Kingdoms in the Precolonial
Period*.

The
New
Oxford
World
History

Forthcoming Titles